Managing Workplace Chaos

Managing Workplace Chaos

Solutions for Handling Information, Paper, Time, and Stress

Patricia J. Hutchings

AMACOM

American Management Association

New York • Atlanta • Brussels • Buenos Aires • Chicago • London • Mexico City
San Francisco • Shanghai • Tokyo • Toronto • Washington, D.C.

This publication is designed to provide accurate and authoritative information in regard to the subject matter covered. It is sold with the understanding that the publisher is not engaged in rendering legal, accounting, or other professional service. If legal advice or other expert assistance is required, the services of a competent professional person should be sought.

Library of Congress Cataloging-in-Publication Data

Hutchings, Patricia J., 1966–
    Managing workplace chaos : solutions for handling information, paper, time, and stress / Patricia J. Hutchings.
        p. cm.
    Includes index.
    ISBN 0-8144-7127-7 (pbk.)
        1. Paperwork (Office practice)—Management. 2. Time management.
    3. Stress management. I. Title.

    HF5547.15 .H88 2002
    650.1—dc21   2001053480

Printing number
10 9 8 7 6 5 4 3

Dedication

To my father for showing me how to be a teacher.
To my husband Bob for believing in me.

Contents

Acknowledgments

I want to acknowledge my mother, Sunny Schneider, for her many contributions to this book. She was my first editor and an advisor throughout the process. I would also like to thank the members of my mastermind group who supported me all the way with their encouragement. They tell me over and over again that I can accomplish whatever I set out to do. I'd also like to thank Andrea Iadanza and Mico Zinty at American Management Association and Ellen Kadin at AMACOM for their support of me and of my work. And last, but most important, the participants in my workshops and seminars who have asked for this book, and for whom the book is written. Every day I learn from you. This book is my gift in return.

How to Use This Book

Stop!

Before you read any further, I want you to think about your purpose in reading this book.

Are you looking for a few tips about ways to reduce stress? Manage time? Read faster?

Do you want to learn it all?

Your purpose will determine how you use this book. Now, whatever your purpose, I want you to preview this book by doing the following things:

Go back to the Table of Contents.

Run your finger under each line.

Notice what each part contains.

If there is a part that attracts you, go to it.

If not, start at the beginning.

Now skim through the pages while noticing main headings.

Use your hand to brush across the page as your gaze follows it.

Notice the preview points at the beginning of each chapter.

Notice all the headings and subheadings. Let your eyes catch a few words here and there.

Do this through the entire book or in the chapters that interest you.

When you are finished, think about the material.

Did you learn anything?

Is there a part that you want to learn more about?

Go back to it and begin to read it through.

When you are finished, try to recall the main points.

Did you miss something?

Go back and check it out.

Do this thinking, checking process until you feel that you have a firm grasp of the material and can restate it in your own words.

Good job. You've learned one of the most important skills of advanced reading.

This book is set up to be read similar to the way that I teach my students in advanced reading to approach a book. In advanced reading, we learn to overview, preview, read, postview, and set up a memory tree for recalling information.

Overview and Preview

As you noticed when you previewed this book, each chapter has preview points at the beginning rather than a summary at the end. In advanced reading, we learn to preview a text before we read it, thereby preparing our minds for what we are about to read. Previewing helps by enhancing our focus and concentration, thereby making our minds more receptive to the information.

Memory Trees

I have also placed a memory tree (a diagram of the main points) at the beginning of each chapter. The memory tree is a visual tool that cements information in our memories and helps us to recall it at will. Adding a visual component to our note taking is similar to showing a person a map while using words to describe a location. It engages both hemispheres of the brain and provides two methods for remembering. The visual anchors the written word and shows the relationship of the information. In Chapter 3, you will learn how to create your own memory trees to help you recall what you have learned.

Read and Practice

Within the text are practice tests, examples, and quizzes that will teach you new skills, show you how other people have used these materials, and show you where you fall in categories such as comprehension, burnout, and stress levels.

Postview and Recall— Memory Trees Revisited

At the end of each chapter, there is a memory tree for readers to complete so that they can jot down what they have learned from the material. In order to remember and recall information, it is important to think about it and to rephrase it *in your own words*. This procedure makes the material yours.

Review

Chapter 10 provides a review of the entire book, a few practice exercises, and a goal-setting grid to take you to the next step in improving your work or personal life.

At the end of my workshops, I usually give my students homework that will take them to the next step in their endeavors to improve their work lives. In the Chapter 10 section Plan and Apply, there are a few applications that will help you to take your next step.

All the stories used throughout the book are real, except that the identities and names have been changed to protect privacy.

What Is Chaos?

Exactly what does chaos look like in today's workplace? I gathered lists of definitions from hundreds of people during my training programs and seminars. Many participants said that chaos is:

Not being able to finish one project before being given another . . . too many people to support . . . lack of communication . . . constant interruptions . . . self-imposed versus real expectations . . . loss of control over work . . . poor time management . . . too many priorities . . . lack of organizational skills . . . too many bosses . . . no downtime . . . no precise job description . . . not knowing what is expected of you . . . harder not smarter . . . office politics . . . too much to do and too little time or too few people to do it . . . lack of direction . . . procrastination . . . immediate demands . . . no enthusiasm . . . E-mail demanding immediate attention . . . mental overload . . . scheduling multiple people for multiple meetings . . . bringing personal problems to work . . . critical coworker . . . inability to focus . . . inability to say no . . . equipment failures . . . traffic . . . inconsistent workload.

Whew! And there is more, but you get the idea. Does any of this sound familiar? I sometimes feel overwhelmed just reading the list.

Introduction

The quantity of information that today's office worker must deal with on a daily basis has grown exponentially. The increasing pace, the rate of change, and the availability and accessibility of new information have become overwhelming—and things are on the verge of exploding! In my workshops and seminars, I meet hundreds of people a week who have similar complaints, and the complaints grow stronger each year. There is an increasing demand for skills, not theories, to help them cope with the onslaught of new technology and information.

Over time, I have found that the areas of immediate concern to workers are managing information, time, and stress. People repeatedly come to me for practical, real-life solutions. In this book, you will find innovative and effective strategies, tools, and skills to help you dig out from underneath your work overload, and to help you flourish instead of flounder in your working environment.

Advanced Reading

Part 1 teaches a skill that I call advanced reading, which is a skill that we are not taught in school. Unfortunately, our schools stop teaching reading at a very elementary level—pun intended. Historically, our schools were established to provide a basic education for a populace that would be capable of working in the newly industrialized society. It was not desired that people learn to question authority, think creatively, or think for themselves. Uniformity and basic literacy were the goals rather than mastery and true literacy. Unfortunately, this tradition has continued up to the present time. Most of our schools stop teaching reading skills after the third grade.

To become an advanced reader, a person must go beyond learning mere word recognition and reading pages word by word, or line by line. Our minds can take in groups of words at a glance and our comprehension increases the faster we read. By using the hand as pacers to draw our vision across and down the page, we can increase our focus and comprehension. In this book, you will learn how to use this skill, in addition to previewing and making memory trees. And you will learn to think about what you have read and to make it your own.

Many of these techniques have existed since ancient times, yet our schools rarely teach them. In the few schools that do teach these skills, test results show amazing advancement in the students' comprehension skills. With a little practice, you can become an advanced reader, too. You'll find that you can deal with your work reading much more efficiently and never again be at the mercy of your information.

Time Perspectives

In Part 2, we take a look at how we use our time. We learn skills to make time our own—instead of being at the mercy of other people. For many of us, the days and weeks go by faster all the time, yet we feel no closer to our goals.

So how do we get a handle on time? First, we discover our values and priorities. We discover what is important to us and to our businesses. Then, from the point of view of these priorities, we set goals. Without goals we are rudderless, but with goals we can find direction and measure our progress.

Once we have some sense of our goals, we look at planning and productivity—again with our values as the foundation. Then, we examine how we organize our space. And finally, we look at our communication skills and ability to be assertive. If we allow it to happen, other people can waste a large amount of our time. We learn how to say no in a polite way—and to mean it.

Finding Balance

In Part 3, we look at ways to create balance in our lives. We take a series of tests to show us where we might be stressed, and learn about the burnout cycle and how to pull ourselves out of it. Participants in my workshops are often surprised at the number of stressors they have in their lives. Even a happy event such as marriage, the birth of a baby, or a job promotion is a major stressor. Stress is not necessarily bad. Life is a dynamic balancing act of stability versus change. The only time that stress is completely absent is when we are dead!

Application Strategies

And finally in Chapter 10, we look at a few application strategies. How do we plan to use what we have learned? We pick our favorite techniques and set up goals for using them.

It is possible to dig ourselves out of the chaos in our work lives. Once we decide that we are in charge, we can make changes that will enhance our lives every day. Start wherever you feel attracted to the information. Will you speed up your reading, organize your space, start looking at your values, or understand how stress plays a part in your life? I invite you to begin today.

PART ONE

Advanced Reading and Recall—Keeping Up with the Twenty-First Century

Information overload is a major cause of stress in the workplace today, and the skill of advanced reading is one of the best time and information management tools you can acquire to alleviate overload. Not only do we have all the stacks of paper that dominate our work spaces, we have the cluttered e-mail and voice mail boxes, along with access to the largest amount of data ever—the World-Wide Web. What do we do with all that data that comes streaming into our offices and homes ending up in stacks on the desks, floors, and overloaded in our computer files? We say, "We'll get to it tomorrow, when we have more time." Right?

Most people I meet and work with rarely, if ever, find "more time," and the stacks continue to grow until most, if not all, the information is obsolete. Meanwhile, their stress level grows along with their fear of not keeping up in their field of expertise. By the time people come to me, they often feel entirely buried under the weight of paper and information! Luckily, all is not lost. They can indeed dig themselves out from whatever data comes their way, and so can you. In this section, I will discuss the skills of advanced reading that allow you to read more quickly (up to ten times faster), learn *what* to read, *how* to read it, and how to *recall* what you have read.

Once you have mastered the skills of advanced reading, you will no longer feel at the mercy of those stacks of papers and waiting e-mails. Information will become a tool that you can use rather than a whirl of chaos burying you.

Do not underestimate the importance of advanced reading in solving the critical time management problem of information flow. While many issues involving time management are not under your direct control, how you manage paper and information is. I have addressed the skills of advanced reading first, because I know of no other skill that can upgrade your efficiency as effectively. It can save you up to 50 percent of the time you now spend on dealing with information and paper.

Upgrade Your Reading Ability

Preview Points

- Determine your reading rate.
- Explore reading definitions.
- Learn how we become linear-subvocal readers.
- Determine how we develop bad reading habits.
- Identify rapid reading potentials.
- Experiment with using a pacer for more effective reading.
- Learn the ideal ergonomics for your work space.

The process of how to read effectively has been known for centuries, even back to the Greek philosopher Socrates. Evelyn Wood, the founder of Evelyn Wood Reading Dynamics, brought the skills into popular culture in the 1960s. By observing naturally rapid readers she developed a method to teach poor readers to excel in reading and in their ability to learn. In the years since then, many teachers have designed courses and books for every level of reader. Yet most people, if they are aware of what is commonly called speed-reading, think of it as a fad or a possibility

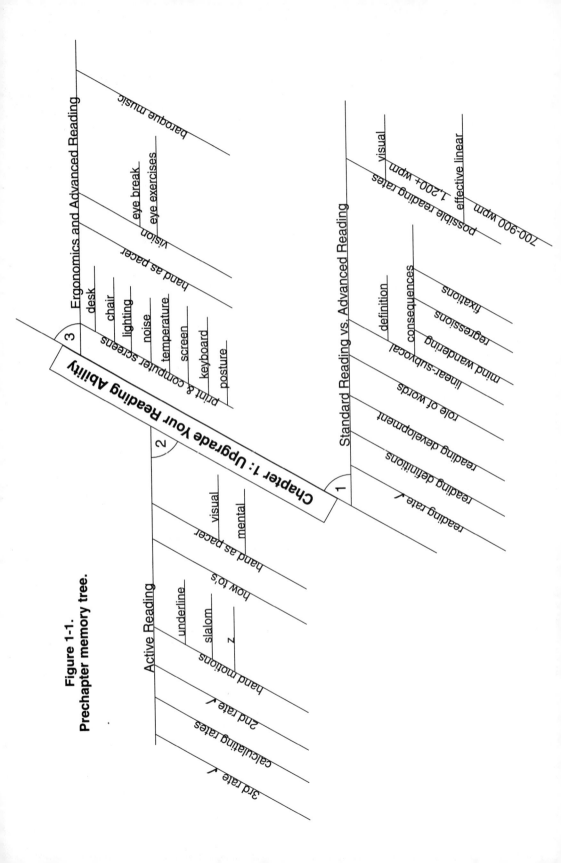

Figure 1-1.
Prechapter memory tree.

Chapter 1: Upgrade Your Reading Ability

Active Reading

- how to's
  - hand as pacer
    - visual
    - mental
  - hand motions
    - underline
    - slalom
    - z
- calculating rates
  - 2nd rate ↗
  - 3rd rate ↗

reading rate ↗

Standard Reading vs. Advanced Reading

- reading definitions
- reading development
- role of words
  - linear-subvocal
  - mind wandering
    - definition
    - consequences
      - fixations
      - regressions
- possible reading rates
  - visual
  - 1,200+ wpm
  - effective linear
  - 700-900 wpm

Ergonomics and Advanced Reading

- print & computer screens
  - desk
  - chair
  - lighting
  - noise
  - temperature
  - screen
  - keyboard
  - posture
- vision
  - hand as pacer
  - eye break
  - eye exercises
- baroque music

limited to only a few, exceptional people. In actuality, with training and practice, anyone can become a more effective reader. The
methods and skills are simple and available to us all.

Standard Reading vs. Advanced Reading

How fast do you read? Do you know? As we begin to explore
improving your reading and information management skills, it
will be helpful for you to know your current reading rate. Time
yourself for one minute while reading the following text and
place a mark where you finish.

Relief from Eyestrain

Today, eyestrain from using computers is becoming so
common that it has been given a name:
Computer Vision Syndrome (CVS). At most workplaces, people
spend hours reading mail and memos, or staring
at computer screens. By the time young people
finish college, 60 to 80 percent are nearsighted.
And people are needing reading glasses at younger and younger
ages. Symptoms of CVS are tired, itchy, or
burning eyes; blurred vision; headache; sore neck; difficulty
focusing; and increased sensitivity to light. Eyestrain is
preventable and correctable if you learn some simple
techniques for eye care. Learn to recognize the
symptoms of eyestrain, and take a break as
soon as you feel any strain. If you
begin taking care of your eyes, you will
never again feel the symptoms of CVS. Here
are some preventative exercises that you can try:

■ Keeping your eyes open, cup them with the
palms of your hands to block out all

light. Rest them in the darkness for at least a minute. Rest your elbows on your desk so that you do not strain your neck and shoulders. Resting your eyes in the darkness allows them to recover from overuse.

■ Roll your eyes clockwise and then counter clockwise, as though you were tracing the outline of a large beach ball. Then pretend that you are looking at a large clock on the wall. Look back and forth from 12:00 to 6:00, 3:00 to 9:00, 11:00 to 5:00 and 1:00 to 7:00. Our eyes are designed to be in constant movement. Staring for long periods of time is very stressful. By exercising our eyes periodically, we relieve the strain of focusing for long periods of time.

■ When you are reading or staring at a computer screen, change your focal point every twenty minutes. Look off into the distance for at least twenty seconds. Staring is hard on the eyes. You can buy a computer program that reminds you to look up from your work at regular intervals. You will be able to work successfully for longer periods of time if you give yourself frequent "eye breaks." Notice whether you are squinting or frowning at the book or computer screen. Consciously relax your facial muscles. Notice whether your neck or back feels strained. Stretch your arms out to the sides and up over your head. Do some head rolls. Flex

your fingers and then make a fist. The
entire body is interconnected. For example, if you
are straining your eyes, chances are you are
building up tension in your neck and shoulder
muscles. Once you become aware of the symptoms
of eyestrain and begin to do these simple
exercises, they will start to become automatic. Neck
hurt? Do some head rolls. Eyes blurry? Palm
them. You will discover that you can work
comfortably for longer periods of time when you
take care of your eyes. The first step
is awareness. Then take action. Our eyes are
designed to be in constant motion. Take frequent
breaks and you will prevent or relieve eyestrain.

©2000 Sunny Schneider, Unique Perspectives Un-Limited, Inc.
Reprinted with permission.

Now count up the number of lines you read. Multiply the number of lines by eight (this article has been printed with an average of eight words per line) to determine how many words per minute you read. For example, let's say I read 30 lines and 3 words on the line where I stopped reading. My rate would be 30 x 8 = 240 + 3 = 243 words per minute (wpm). You may want to jot this number down on your Reading Drill Log at the back of the book.

Now you know how fast you read. To put that into perspective, know that the average reading rates in the United States range from 150 to 400 wpm. Why such a range? There are many reasons, which include level of education, enjoyment or lack of enjoyment of reading, the process by which you were taught to read, how much punishment you received about learning reading skills, whether school in general and reading in particular were valued in the environment where you grew up, whether you were read to as a child, or whether you were told that you were a bad or slow reader.

How long have you been reading the way you read right now? For most of us, it has been since the sixth grade. Rarely are we taught the skill of reading beyond that point. Many of us are familiar with the common theory that the average U.S. reader reads at the sixth-grade level. This statistic generally refers to *vocabulary level*. What we will be exploring in this book is the *skill* of reading. Building vocabulary is always a good idea, however, it is not our focus.

Our focus in Part 1 is to explore how we were trained to read compared to what we are capable of accomplishing.

Reading Definitions

Let's take a look at what reading means, and then explore how most of us were taught to read. We will discuss the consequences of that training and what you can do to become a more advanced reader.

I use the term *advanced reading* as opposed to speed-reading for a number of reasons. I believe that anyone can improve his or her reading ability no matter how well or poorly he or she reads now. Also, I have found that most people I talk to have their own beliefs and comfort levels when it comes to reading. They find it easier to accept that they can improve their skills rather than become a speed-reader. And last, the term *speed-reading* encourages the bad habit of reading for speed instead of content. As an advanced reader, you will indeed read faster, but only as a byproduct of reading more effectively.

It is difficult to find an exact definition of reading, but the following will give us a framework of understanding how the developed skill of reading differs from our current or common understanding of reading.

The *Webster's College Dictionary* defines reading as "to look at so as to understand the meaning of something printed."[1]

The definitions that I developed to define reading are:

■ ***Reading is the interaction between you and the printed text.*** This definition is common to those who love to read. Do you remember the best book you ever read? Did you get so caught up in the story that you lost a sense of place and time? Or couldn't put the book down? This is how reading is meant to be—your mind and the author's mind communicating via the words on a page. You can get lost in the story!

■ *Reading is the process of purposefully and actively seeking meaning and understanding from the written work.* I feel that this definition is appropriate for business reading. Because of our early reading training, we tend to be passive readers rather than being purposeful and active when we read. We look at the words but do not absorb what they are saying to us, so we read them over and over again. We will explore techniques to become more active and deliberate while reading.

These definitions describe reading as a mental or thinking process rather than the mere recognition of words. In advanced reading you go to the next step, beyond what you probably learned in school. Let's now examine how most of us were taught to read and how that has limited our ability to keep up with information chaos.

Reading Skill Development

The way that we were taught to read greatly influences how effective we are now. No matter what your reading background, you can learn to read more effectively. Reading is a skill, not an inborn talent. Just like any skill, with practice and the right techniques you can improve.

Reading development follows a fairly similar process for all of us. We begin with the alphabet, which we memorize. We then begin to learn sound and word formation and begin sounding out words in text. For example, the word *cat* is pronounced as three distinct sounds, or c-a-t. Next, we start working on early reader books and most likely receive spelling tests. At some point around the first grade, we are asked to read aloud. Once it has been established that we can "read" by saying the words aloud, we are then asked to read *silently to ourselves*. This is a key moment.

Most of us, as children, do not understand figurative speech. We take things literally. So as early readers, we quite literally read silently to ourselves. To this day, in many third and fourth grade classrooms, we can observe children reading and see their lips move as they go along. I still see many adults today doing the same thing. This ties our reading speed to our speech rate. So, we read only as fast as we can sound out words silently to ourselves. This is called *subvocalization.*

Many of you may remember the Federal Express® commercial a number of years ago with the man speaking extremely fast. It has been estimated that he was speaking at 436 words per minute! Most of us cannot speak that quickly out loud, but our vocal folds are capable of vibrating that quickly when we are reading silently to ourselves. This is why we have reading rates in the 400 wpm range even when the reader is subvocalizing. The average reader today reads around 200 to 250 wpm.

A misconception that slows our reading is the belief that we need to say a word to ourselves to understand its meaning. This makes sense to many of us because, from the time we were very little, we have been sounding out words in our minds. This is what we are comfortable with. Learning to pronounce words is important for conversing in a language. It is a key component in vocabulary development, but *it is not reading.*

Once we learn a word, we no longer need to say it to ourselves. Yet, many of us get stuck here. In most of our daily routines, we do not say words to ourselves. We read road signs, packaging, and look over papers very effectively without subvocalizing. For most of us, it is only when we think that we must "read" that we fall into old, trained habits. Learning to read by sight is a skill you can develop and use all the time. It is similar to going from c-a-t to cat to knowing what the animal is without saying it to yourself at all.

The Role of Words in Reading

At this point it may be helpful to understand the role of words in the reading process. When reading, individual words do not carry meaning, however, groups of words do. It is the relationship of words to each other that combine to create meaning for us.

For the most part, we were taught language skills in school such as spelling, pronunciation, grammar, and word usage. All of these are important, but they do not constitute reading. To illustrate what I mean, think about a foreign language class you took in high school. If I handed you a book in that language, could you read it? More than likely, you could not. Even when you were taking the class, did you learn to read? Or did you learn to *translate*? Much like we were taught in English, our foreign language teachers gave us word lists for learning the correct spelling, pronunciation, English meaning, and grammatical usage. To understand a new language, most of us have to convert the language back to our primary language to understand the meaning—and meaning is what reading is all about.

When we were taught to read, most likely we were being taught language skills. Comprehension was somehow supposed to occur on its own. Some schools have formal reading classes in the early grades that teach reading comprehension, and students who are exposed to theses classes tend to be on the upper end of reading abilities later in life.

There is a major difference between seeing words and understanding their meaning. Keep in mind words are symbols. We do not think in words, we think in pictures, concepts, and ideas. Individual words are simply symbols that can have many different meanings, or carry no meaning on their own, or even have the meanings change over time! Many people find that although they see words and even sound them out in their minds, their recall of the information these words convey is poor if not absent altogether.

Reading subvocally is a four-step process:

1. See a word.

2. Say it to ourselves.

3. Hear the word in our minds.

4. Understand what the word is.

Advanced reading involves removing steps two and three, so that we rely on our sight instead of our hearing to accept words into our minds. Ideally, we move from the four-step process to a two-step process:

1. *See* a word.

2. *Know* what it represents.

Moving from the four-step to the two-step process is a skill that develops through drilling and practice, and is the step that is missing from most traditional reading training.

Linear-Subvocal Reading

The average person in the United States is considered a *linear-subvocal* reader. We just explored the subvocal issue as a leftover habit from our early reading training. Also note that what we are taught is not wrong or bad, only that we are not taught beyond this level, which holds us back. Our training ends too soon.

Next, let's explore the linear part of linear-subvocal. Do you see linearly? Do your eyes scan in narrow bands from top to bottom? No! However, because we were trained to focus on words printed linearly from left to right, we make our eyes constrict to follow that pattern. In order to say the sounds, our eyes had to see them. Therefore, we only focused on one word at a time. Reading this way is tiring for most people because the eye muscles contract or fixate for each word or small word group.

As adults, eye fixations occur when we read because we are still trying to focus on one word at a time, no matter how small the print is. This causes a great deal of eyestrain and eye damage for many people. Fixations are like skipping movements across a line. It is estimated that our eyes skip and jump three to six times per line. This can use up to 25 percent of our reading time that could be better spent.

One of the main benefits of advanced reading skills is the shift in how we use our eyes. Instead of attempting to fix our eyes on each word, we learn to use a more relaxed and natural focus.

This allows us to read more comfortably for longer periods of time and diminishes eyestrain.

Two of the negative consequences of being a linear-subvocal reader are that the mind wanders and we frequently read the same material over and over, thereby making our reading extremely inefficient.

Mind Wandering

How many of you find your mind wandering while you read? My guess is that many—if not all—of you sometimes find it difficult to keep your mind on your reading. This is normal given our current approach to reading. Reading at a slow, plodding pace and having no focus for your reading encourages the mind to take frequent side trips.

How many of you have had the following experience: You sit down to read something important. You start at the beginning, saying words to yourself, turning pages, just like always. Three to four pages into the material your mind is in Hawaii— you're on a mental vacation. Or maybe you're thinking about an important presentation coming up in the afternoon. Whatever it is you're daydreaming about—your mind is gone. Yet, you are most likely still going through the motions of reading (saying words to yourself and turning pages) without really processing the words on the page.

Do you notice when your mind wanders? Usually not until you come back from the mental vacation. Mind wandering can last up to ten minutes in a one-hour period. I think our minds say, "You know, you said this was boring and you don't like reading it and gave me no reason to remember it. So, you sit there and talk to yourself while I go and think about all this other stuff we've got going on right now." And that is exactly what it does.

Mind wandering can also occur when we are multitasking. We are attempting to do too many things at one time. When you are reading something that is important to you, your focus must be 100 percent on the material at hand.

In this chapter, we will discuss using a pacer to help you stay focused. In Chapter 2, we will explore purposeful reading techniques to further that focus. Part 2 will help you to deal with the multitasking issue.

The Importance of Break Time

If we are to dig ourselves out from under the chaos at work, we must learn that we actually get more work done when we take frequent breaks.

A break can be as simple as looking up from your papers or the computer screen and allowing your eyes to focus on some point in the distance. At the same time, you could take some deep breaths, stretch out your arms to each side and then above your head. When you stretch, you usually make a sound such as a groan or sigh. Making sound is a natural stress reliever.

Any time your mind starts to wander or you feel cramped or fatigued, remember to take a short break. Then, at least once an hour, get up from your desk and take a short walk, while stretching, sighing (this can be done very quietly under your breath), and taking some deep breaths. A ten-minute break is best. You will come back to your work energized and able to concentrate much better than if you ignore your body's needs. In business and life, we often let our minds overrule our bodies, leading to overload and stress. Advanced reading will make you more efficient in your processing of written material so that you can afford to take frequent breaks.

Frequent breaks are especially crucial when you are working at a computer. Because such a large number of people are having back, shoulder, neck, wrist, and hand pain from sitting at a computer and keyboarding for extended periods of time, laws are being written to guarantee workers ergonomically supportive workstations. Doctors warn about repetitive strain injuries. Be aware of your body's signals and heed them. When you need to think, get up and pace the office rather than sitting immobile in your chair.

If you normally become so involved in your work that you forget to take breaks, here are two tricks to try. If you are reading a book, make a bookmark and place it several pages ahead in the book. When you come to the bookmark, take a break. Look up, breathe, stretch, sigh, and relax. If you are at the computer, there are programs you can buy that will flash a message on your screen telling you to take a break. You set the program for the time interval you want. Again, look up, breathe, stretch, sigh, and relax. (Try typing the word *ergonomics* into your search engine to find one of these programs.)

Reading Regressions

Reading regressions occur when we find ourselves rereading the same material. We can do this anywhere from ten to thirteen times per every one hundred words we read. Most frequently, reading regressions are caused by a lack of purpose in reading. Have you ever found yourself reading and rereading something because you don't know what you're looking for, or even looking at? When we do not have a purpose, we may know the words, but not what they represent, so our mind retraces the text to search for meaning.

The advanced reading technique eliminates the problems of subvocalization, mind wandering, and regression. We learn that reading is an active and deliberate process. To keep up with the twenty-first century, it is necessary to become an advanced reader to get ahead. Let's look at the possibilities.

How Fast Can You Read?

Before we explore how fast you need to read, let's first look at what is possible. It has been estimated that the average person can think at 50,000 wpm or more. Although we may not be able to read this fast physically, our minds are capable of processing much more than 150 to 400 wpm. In fact, the mind stays much better engaged when we read closer to our mental capacity. Remember in school when your class would take turns reading a story aloud? Did you sometimes become impatient and read ahead? Your mind wanted to leap ahead to find out what was going to happen.

Some people are naturally effective readers. They never developed the habit of subvocalization. For example, John F. Kennedy was a naturally advanced reader who brought teachers from the Evelyn Wood organization to the White House to teach his staff speed reading skills. The nineteenth-century English philosopher and economist John Stuart Mill's main complaint was not being able to turn pages quickly enough. Howard Stephen Berg holds the record as the world's fastest reader[2] for reading more than 20,000 words per minute with full comprehension.

Others, while not naturally advanced readers, have used various methods to train themselves to be more effective. Many of my colleagues at the Evelyn Wood organization read in the thousands of words per minute, all of whom were trained in her methods. Others have read books or attended classes to improve their skills, and some fortunate people were even taught in school!

The reading rate of *visual* readers (people who read groups of words across and down the page without subvocalizing) is 1,200 to 1,500 wpm. It takes a minimum of three weeks of drilling and training for most linear-subvocal readers to retrain themselves to this level.

The upper limit of effective *linear* reading, in which the reader reads left to right, line by line, is 700 to 900 wpm. People who read at 200+ wpm can develop their skills to this level with practice and a new approach. I will discuss the approach and give practice drills and tips in the remainder of Part 1.

So, how fast do you need to read? To keep up with today's streaming level of data, I suggest a minimum of 800 to 1,000 wpm. But you need to be the ultimate judge. Even if you only double your current rate, you will get through your reading in 50 percent less time than before. If you include the additional techniques of comprehension and memory, your effectiveness will improve ten-fold. This is the best time management tool that I know of.

Remember, using numbers is merely a way to describe reading levels. The goal is not speed, but effectiveness. By being an effective reader, you will naturally begin to read faster.

Understand that reading is more than identifying and sounding out letters and words on a page. It is about interpreting groups of words to gain meaning. To do this we need to use our eyes and mind differently.

Active Reading

So far, I have discussed the need to turn reading into an active and deliberate process. Now we will explore the techniques you need to become an advanced reader.

The two core skills of an effective reader are using a pacer to read and purposeful reading.

Using the Hand as a Visual and Mental Pacer

A core skill in advanced reading is using a pacer. A pacer is any object that helps you follow along the lines or page while reading. Many devices have been invented over the years to use as a pacer, but you already have the best device attached to your body—your hand.

The use of a pacer provides rhythm and movement. Without this guide, the eyes tend to move randomly and uncontrollably over the lines of print. The pacer helps to eliminate regressions and fixations. The use of the hand is also important as a training device to help decrease the subvocalization that occurs with traditional reading behavior. As we draw our hand across the page smoothly and quickly, it is harder to say all the words under our breath, and eventually we stop. The use of the hand enhances concentration and, when used in a conscious manner, provides a wider range of flexibility of rates when reading.

Initially, using your hand as a pacer may feel challenging. When we were taught to read in school, many of us were told not to point to words or to use our hands. My students even report that they were told that they were stupid if they used their hands. Some were physically punished. Luckily, many reading teachers today realize the benefits of utilizing the hand as a pacer. Just remember, you do not want to point to each word. Keep the hand movement smooth across the lines of type.

It will take only a few hours before using a pacer starts to become second nature. Soon you will notice how your reading slows and you become distracted every time you stop using your hand—and how your focus and speed increase when you use it. You will find, with practice, that the motion of the hand fades into the background like the windshield wipers on your car. The wipers move across your vision, but you look beyond them.

To understand how a pacer improves the eyes' movement, try this experiment. Ask a friend to sit or stand facing you. Have your friend slowly move his or her eyes in a circular motion, as if tracing the outline of a large beach ball that is suspended in the air between the two of you. What do your friend's eyes do? Does it look like he or she is tracing a beach ball? Or does it look more like a stop sign? Now have your friend use his or her eyes to follow your hand as you trace the imaginary beach ball in the air between you. What did you notice about your friend's eye movement this time? His or her eyes made a smooth circle, didn't they? This is how using a pacer assists you when you are reading, by smoothing out your eye movements.

Another way to understand how you are attempting to use your eyes is to imagine how your eyes function naturally. Imagine window-shopping as you walk down a busy city street. You are aware of the other pedestrians and their movements, the street vendors, the traffic, the items displayed in the windows, and the SALE signs. You also notice, while dodging a dog walker with an out-of-control dog, a lovely pink sweater with rhinestone buttons and satin trim that would be just perfect for . . . *You see and understand all of this and more*! You notice the condition of the sidewalk and admire some trees and flowers—all while walking.

Our goal in reading is to see all of the words as our vision passes over them and to allow our minds to absorb the meaning and significance of the words—similar to finding that perfect gift while window-shopping. We have a purpose as our eyes "walk through the words," and that purpose keeps us focused on finding the information we seek. There may be much extraneous information in the written material, but our purpose allows us to extract what we are seeking from what (to us) is merely scenery.

How to Use the Hand as a Pacer

When using your hand as a pacer, it is important to move your elbow rather than your wrist, and to keep your shoulder dropped and relaxed. Keep your arm straight, from the fingertips to the elbow. Most people use their dominant hand, although you can try either hand to see which one feels the most comfortable.

Use the tips of the fingers to lightly touch the page as they underline the words. You can use your whole hand, your index finger, or index and middle finger with the other fingers tucked in. You can also make an OK sign with thumb and index finger and use the rest of the fingers to brush under the lines. Try several hand configurations to find the one that feels best to you.

When beginning to use a pacer for reading, the temptation is to focus on your hand rather than on the information. An easy way to keep your focus on the text is to ask yourself some questions about what you are reading. This will help you to focus on the meaning of the words instead of on the process of pacing.

It is necessary to insert a word of caution here. Do not try to read quickly or to speed-read. When you do this, your mind is focused on speed and not on comprehension. You may cover all the material quickly, but generally you will not have understood much of what was there. You want to focus your mind on the information. The more focused you are, the faster your mind will naturally move. The temptation is to move the hand quickly to read faster. However, if you do this, you may find that your hand is moving down the page but your eyes are still at the top of the page reading the old way. Strive for coordination between your eye and hand movements.

Most of us will naturally find a comfortable process for pacing, but there are some techniques that will help you to become as effective as possible. These tips are also helpful if you want to teach this method to someone else.

The Underlining Hand Motion

The basic hand motion to begin with is called the underlining hand motion. (See Figure 1-2.) Your hand paces under each line of text exactly as it is printed. Lightly touch the page while underlining the line and lift the hand at the right margin. Return the hand to the next line at the left margin. Lifting the hand off the page at the right margin ensures that the eyes are drawn to that side of the page. The eyes and hand move together over the text. Your mind will determine how fast to go to comfortably comprehend the material.

Figure 1-2.
Underlining hand motion.

qqqq qqqqqqq qqqq qq q qqqq qqq qq
qqqqq qq qqqqqqq qqqqq qqqqqq q qq qqqq qq
qqqq qq qq qq q q q qqqqqq qqqq qqq qqq q qq
q qqq qq qqqq qqqqq qq qq q qqqqq qqqqqq q q.
www ww wwwww www ww w ww
wwww wwww ww w ww wwwwwww ww w w
www www w w w w www ww www w wwww
ww w wwww ww wwww www ww w ww ww
www w ww wwwww ww w wwww www ww
w ww ww ww.
X XXX XX XXXXX XX XXX XXX X XX XXXXX
X XX XXXX XX XX XXXX XX XX XXXXXX X XXX XX X
XXXXXX XXX XXXXXXX XXXX XXX X XX X XXXX
XXX XXX XX XX XXXXXXX X XX XX X X XXX XX XX
XXX XX XX XX XX XX XXXXX XXXXX XX XXX XX XX
XXXX XXXXXX X XX X XXXXXX XXX XXX X X X XXX
XX XX X X XXXXXX XX XXXXX XX XXXXXXXXX XX X
XXXXXX XX X X.
ZZZZ ZZZZ ZZZZ ZZ Z Z ZZZZZ ZZ Z ZZZZZZZ
ZZZZZZ ZZ ZZ Z Z ZZZZ ZZZZZ Z ZZZZZZ ZZZZZZ ZZ Z
ZZ ZZ Z ZZZZZZZ Z ZZZZ ZZ ZZ ZZZ Z ZZ ZZZZZZZZZZ

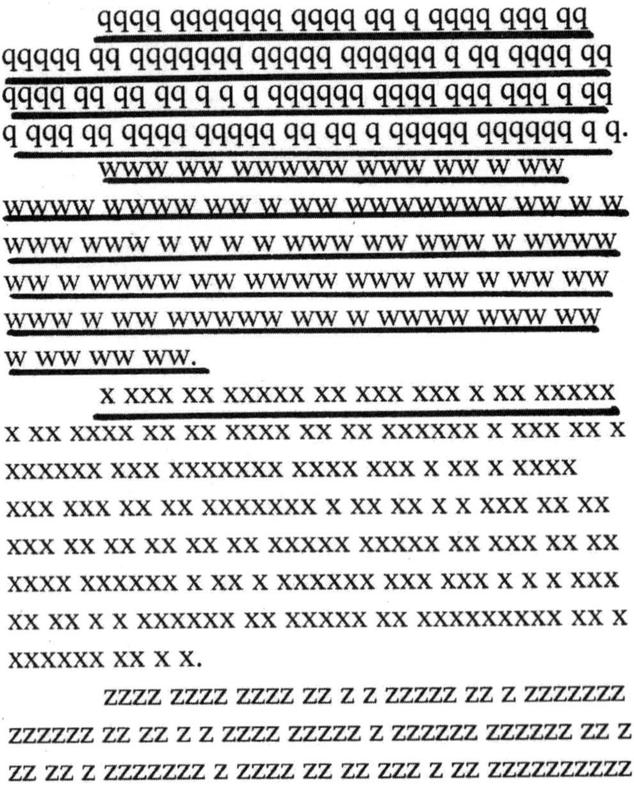

Practice the underlining hand motion on the article below. Again, time yourself for one minute.

The Effects of Environment and Nutrition on Learning

There is a growing body of scientific evidence about the effects of the environment on our ability to learn, from the time we are babies to our old age. It would seem unnecessary to mention how strongly we are affected by our environment, except that we so often ignore our physical surroundings in relationship to ourselves. Our environment affects us! All outer changes affect our physiology. We are always adjusting to what is happening around us.

It has been discovered that our brain waves react to our surroundings. They synchronize with each other (a state more receptive to learning) when we look at a scene in nature. They do not when we look at an industrial scene or even at a parking lot. Natural light and full-spectrum lighting are better for us than fluorescent light. The flickering of fluorescent lights interferes with our concentration and can cause hyperactivity. Rock-and-roll music or any jarring music makes our cells jumpy. Classical music soothes our cells. Some foods help balance our bodies and increase our ability to learn. Other foods put us out of balance and can interfere with concentration. Since we are life-long learners, it makes sense to pay attention to these environmental factors that can help or hinder the process.

How many of us drink a cup of
coffee and eat a pastry or muffin for
breakfast? How many of us skip breakfast altogether?
I recently had a participant in one of
my seminars who was so tired she had
to put her head down on the table
at 2:30 P.M., causing her to miss critical
pieces of the program. This woman had consumed
a soft drink, corn chips, and a cookie
that day. What is wrong with this picture?

There are many opinions about the best type
of breakfast, but most agree that we need
protein to sustain energy. Sugar burns up quickly
then lets us down. We are all familiar
with a sugar rush after eating too many
sweets. Sugar is used up quickly or turns
to fat.

Our brains need adequate, high-quality protein to function.
Protein is the main building block of our
cells. It is best to eat small amounts
of whole protein foods spread out through our
meals during the day. Too much protein at
once can be hard to digest. Also, as
we get older, we do not have as
much stomach acid and digestive enzymes to digest
protein easily. If this is true for you,

it is a good idea to take a
supplement containing enzymes just before or after eating.
Vegetarians can eat soy or rice protein, but
the body finds it harder to extract protein
from fibrous foods, so digestive enzymes can help
there, too. Raw vegetables are a good source
of natural enzymes. (Cooking destroys enzymes.) A diet
of high-quality protein, lots of raw vegetables,
and a moderate amount of grains seems to
be best for our brains as well as
our bodies.

Vitamin B12, lecithin, and all the B vitamins
are necessary for brain functions. Lecithin has been
shown to have a remarkable ability to increase
memory and learning ability. B vitamins can be
taken in supplements or are found in eggs,
fish, lean beef, wheat, and soy beans.

An herb that is receiving much press for
brain functioning is Ginkgo biloba. It helps blood
flow throughout the body and specifically to the
brain, thereby helping to oxygenate the brain. European
medicine has used Ginkgo biloba for many years
in the treatment of senile dementia and even
Alzheimer's disease. Information on these substances can
be found at health food stores, in magazines
such as *Prevention* and *Alternative Medical Review,* and
even in the *Journal of the American Medical Association.*

Count up the number of lines you read and multiply by eight. Add any additional words beyond a full line. Record this rate in your drill log and compare it to your earlier rate on the same material. Did you read it faster? Did you notice your eyes moving more smoothly?

The Slalom Hand Motion

Now that you have worked with the underlining hand motion, let us look at another way to pace through material. The slalom hand motion is a very fluid motion that many people find them-selves using naturally. (See Figure 1-3.) The main difference between underlining and the slalom movement is that you keep your hand on the page during the back sweep. To use the slalom, underline a line from left to right, then, keeping your hand in con-tact with the page, rapidly sweep your hand back from right to

Figure 1-3.
Narrow slalom.

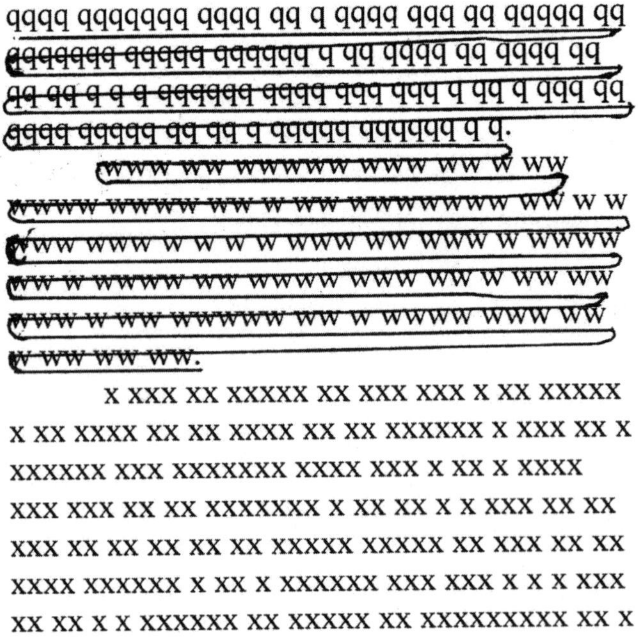

qqqq qqqqqqq qqqq qq q qqqq qqq qq qqqqq qq
qqqqqqq qqqqq qqqqqq q qq qqqq qq qqqq qq
qq qq q q q qqqqqq qqqq qqq qqq q qq q qqq qq
qqqq qqqqq qq qq q qqqqq qqqqqq q q.
www ww wwwww www ww w ww
wwwww wwwww ww w ww wwwwwww ww w w
www wwww w w w w wwww ww wwww w wwwww
ww w wwwww ww wwwww www ww w ww ww
www w ww wwwww ww w wwww www ww
w ww ww ww.

X XXX XX XXXXX XX XXX XXX X XX XXXXX
X XX XXXX XX XX XXXX XX XX XXXXXX X XXX XX X
XXXXXX XXX XXXXXXX XXXX XXX X XX X XXXX
XXX XXX XX XX XXXXXXX X XX XX X X XXX XX XX
XXX XX XX XX XX XX XXXXX XXXXX XX XXX XX XX
XXXX XXXXXX X XX X XXXXXX XXX XXX X X X XXX
XX XX X X XXXXXX XX XXXXX XX XXXXXXXXX XX X

left, then proceed to the next line. Be careful not to let the movement of your hand gravitate to the middle of the text. You want to keep the movement complete from margin to margin so you can see all the words.

In the beginning you may notice the eye/mind picking up words on the back sweep (when you go from right to left). If you find this method to be too distracting, switch back to underlining. Keep in mind that you are not attempting to read backwards.

By using fewer sweeps of the slalom on the page, you can get a larger perspective of the material you are reading. For example, a medium slalom (see Figure 1-4) would help you to focus on

Figure 1-4.
Medium slalom.

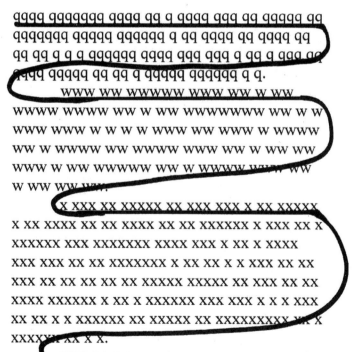

main headings, first and last sentences of paragraphs, and key
words or phrases. Your focus continues to be from left to right on
these targeted sentences.

An open slalom (see Figure 1-5) allows you to survey entire
pages at a time, so that you are able to take a quick inventory of
a book or document to see what it contains and how it is laid out.
Your focus is now on scanning the entire page.

Figure 1-5.
Open slalom.

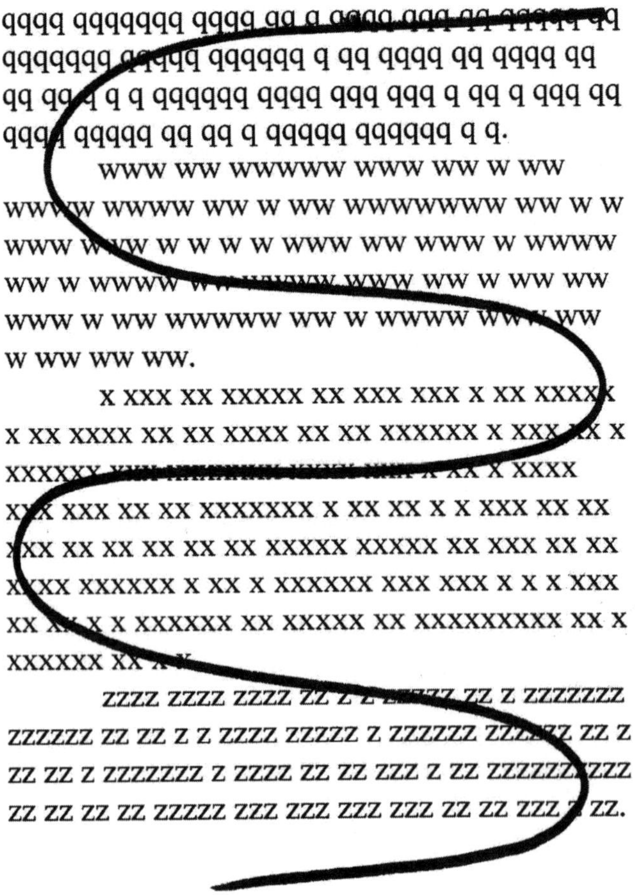

qqqq qqqqqqq qqqq qq q qqqq qqq qq qqqq qq
qqqqqqq qqqqq qqqqqq q qq qqqq qq qqqq qq
qq qq q q q qqqqqq qqqq qqq qqq q qq q qqq qq
qqqq qqqqq qq qq q qqqqq qqqqqq q q.
www ww wwwww www ww w ww
wwww wwww ww w ww wwwwwww ww w w
www w ww w w w w www ww www w wwww
ww w wwww ww wwww www ww w ww ww
www w ww wwwww ww w wwww ww ww
w ww ww ww.
X XXX XX XXXXX XX XXX XXX X XX XXXXX
X XX XXXX XX XX XXXX XX XX XXXXXX X XXX XX X
XXXXXX XXX XX X XX X XXXX
XX XXX XX XX XXXXXXX X XX XX X X XXX XX XX
XXX XX XX XX XX XX XXXXX XXXXX XX XXX XX XX
XXX XXXXXX X XX X XXXXXX XXX XXX X X X XXX
XX XX X X XXXXXX XX XXXXX XX XXXXXXXXX XX X
XXXXXX XX XX
ZZZZ ZZZZ ZZZZ ZZ Z Z ZZZZ ZZ Z ZZZZZZZZ
ZZZZZZ ZZ ZZ Z Z ZZZZ ZZZZZ Z ZZZZZZZ ZZ ZZ ZZ Z
ZZ ZZ Z ZZZZZZZ Z ZZZZ ZZ ZZ ZZZ Z ZZ ZZZZZZ ZZZ
ZZ ZZ ZZ ZZ ZZZZZ ZZZ ZZZ ZZZ ZZZ ZZ ZZ ZZZ Z ZZ.

The Z Hand Motion

The next hand motion to work with is called the Z. (See Figure 1-6.) The Z hand motion combines linear and dimensional hand movements. It is an excellent transitional hand motion for helping you to become comfortable seeing words differently on the page, while allowing you to practice relaxed focus as you read.

To begin, underline the first line on the page from left to right, then slant back through two to four lines on the back sweep. Proceed to underline the next line. Slant back through two to four

Figure 1-6.
Z hand motion.

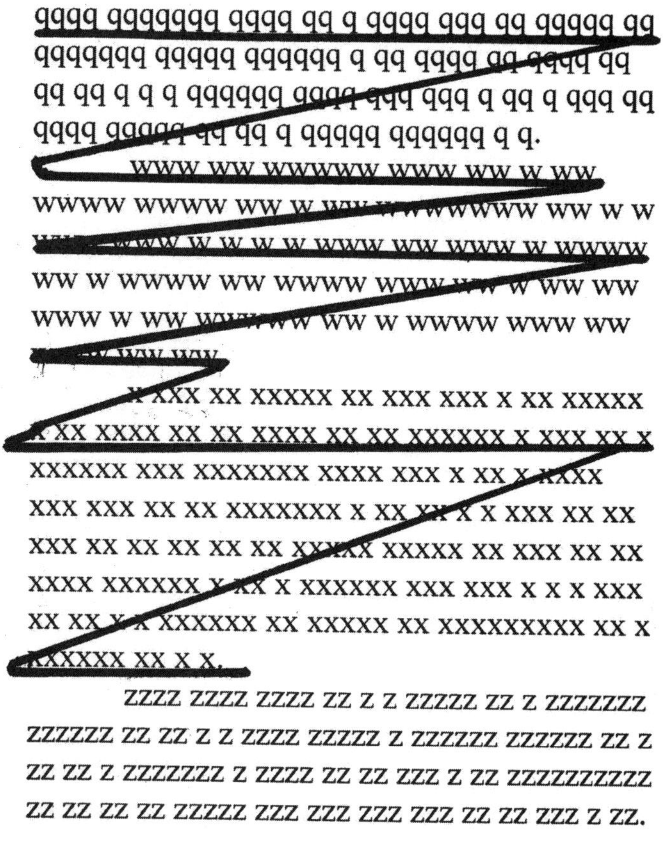

qqqq qqqqqqq qqqq qq q qqqq qqq qq qqqqq qq
qqqqqqq qqqqq qqqqqq q qq qqqq qq qqqq qq
qq qq q q q qqqqqq qqqq qqq qqq q qq q qqq qq
qqqq qqqqq qq qq q qqqqq qqqqqq q q.
www ww wwwww www ww w ww
wwww wwww ww w www www wwwww ww w w
www www w w w w www www wwww w wwwww
ww w wwww ww wwww www w w ww ww
www w ww www ww ww w wwww www ww
www www
x xxx xx xxxxx xx xxx xxx x xx xxxxx
x xx xxxx xx xx xxxx xx xx xxxxxx x xxx xx x
xxxxxx xxx xxxxxxx xxxx xxx x xx x xxxx
xxx xxx xx xx xxxxxxx x xx xx x x xxx xx xx
xxx xx xx xx xx xx xxxxx xxxxx xx xxx xx xx
xxxx xxxxxx x xx x xxxxxx xxx xxx x x x xxx
xx xx x x xxxxxx xx xxxxx xx xxxxxxxxx xx x
xxxxxx xx x x.
zzzz zzzz zzzz zz z z zzzzz zz z zzzzzzz
zzzzzz zz zz z z zzzz zzzzz z zzzzzz zzzzz zz z
zz zz z zzzzzzz z zzzz zz zz zzz z zz zzzzzzzzzz
zz zz zz zz zzzzz zzz zzz zzz zzz zz zz zzz z zz.

more lines. You can open up this hand motion to cover entire paragraphs. Practice using this hand motion on the previous article to get a feel for it. You will notice you get the gist of what you are looking at but not much more—that is great! Over time you may find yourself reading with this hand motion if you practice with it regularly.

Once you have practiced using different hand motions, you are ready to start reading drills.

Reading Drills

Reading drills are the most effective method for improving both the speed at which you read and your comprehension levels. For the best results, it is ideal to complete one or two reading drills per day for three weeks.

The definition of drilling as it relates to reading is using your hand as a pacer to condition yourself to take in many more words at a time, thus improving your concentration and comprehension. Reading drills are used to increase your ability to process more words in less time.

It may feel as though nothing is happening when you first begin to drill. Remember that your mind is stretching and becoming accustomed to this advanced process. Drilling builds the skill of reading, similar to the way practicing your golf or tennis swing improves your game. The practice is not the game and drilling is not the same as reading. However, drilling is a key skill that will turn you into an advanced reader.

Basic Drill Instructions

Establish a starting point in a book and place a paper clip or sticky note there to mark it. Using your hand as a pacer, do a practice read for one minute, pushing yourself to read at a slightly faster rate than normal. Place another marker where you end. Return to your starting point. Practice read again for one minute, pushing yourself faster to get beyond your original ending point. Move your ending marker to your new ending point. Return to your original starting point. Practice read again for one minute, pushing yourself faster to get even further in the material. Move the ending marker to your new ending point.

Count up the number of pages you have covered at this point in the drill. Create a new ending point that is *double* the number of pages you have covered so far. In one minute, pace your vision and practice read to reach your new ending point. With this phase of the drill, you are not attempting to understand all of what you are seeing. You are becoming accustomed to using your hand as a pacer and taking in more words with each glance (see Figure 1-7, Guidelines for Drilling).

Finally, find a new starting point in the middle of the drill pages. Read for comprehension for one minute. Do not push or stretch for speed. Calculate and record your rate using the instructions that follow in "How to Calculate Reading Rates in Any Book."

Figure 1-7.
Guidelines for drilling.

Step Amount of material covered in one minute from original start-ing point

A | — — — — —(slightly faster than comfortable comprehen-sion)—line by line pacing

B | — — — — — — — — — (faster still, usually ½ to 3 pages fur-ther in the text)—line by line pacing

C | — — — — — — — — — — —(even faster! Usually ½ to 2 pages further in the text)—line by line pacing

D | — — — — — — — — — — — — — —(2 x further than step C)—sweeping open slalom pacing

E   (new starting place) | — — — — —............(read for solid comprehension for one minute)—line by line pacing

F   Calculate and record your rate for step E.

You will find that your reading rate increases dramatically with only a few days of practice using the hand as a pacer. By the end of three weeks, you will have become an advanced reader for life. For information on where to order an audiotape that has these instructions timed for you, see the About the Author section at the back of this book.

I recommend that you choose one book in which to do all your reading drills. Ideally, the book will be one you have read before that is written at or below your current vocabulary level. This way you will feel more comfortable pushing yourself through the exercises.

How to Calculate Reading Rates in Any Book

When drilling in a book, you will want to record your reading rates, so you can track your progress over time. Use the following formula to determine your book's average words per page and how to calculate your reading rate:

- Count the number of words on three full lines. Add this up and divide by three. This equals the average number of words per line (wpl).

- Count the number of lines on three average pages. Add this up and divide by three. This equals the average number of lines per page (lpp).

- To determine the average number of words per page (wpp), multiply the average number of words per line times the average number of lines per page (wpl x lpp = wpp).

   For example: 10 wpl x 35 lpp = 350 wpp.

- To determine your average word per minute (wpm) rate: Multiply the average words per page times the number pages read and divide by the amount of minutes you read. For example, let's say you read 4 pages in 3 minutes and the book has an average of 350 words per page. 350 wpp x 4 pages ÷ 3 = 466 wpm.

Check your reading rate after completing a drill. In the book of your choice, complete a reading drill as described in the previous example. When you are finished, read the following article. This article is printed with eight words per line on average, so your calculations will be the same as the earlier exercises in the book.

Early Warning Signs of Burnout

Burnout is very popular today. It is common to hear people in organizations brag about their level of stress and how overworked they are. What I don't see are many people taking steps to take care of themselves and get back on track. Most people seem to expect it all to go away, or they resign themselves to feeling bad. It is important to begin recognizing the early warning signs of stress and burnout and to take steps to bring life into balance before things get worse. We don't have to wait for overwork to put us flat on our backs to wake up to the need to find joy in our lives. If we do, our bodies will continue to up the ante until we pay attention and make some necessary life changes to get back on track. Some early warning signs are as follows. (Keep in mind that some of these behaviors may be normal for you. Be concerned only if they begin to happen more than usual.) Disorganization—You are misplacing things, such as your glasses (and they are on your head); locking your keys in your car; becoming accident prone; bumping into things; losing track

of common items. Dependency—Needing people or comfort
food more than normal, such as eating an
entire quart or gallon of ice cream in
one sitting, making more telephone calls than usual
to friends and family, needing to be connected
all the time, getting overly emotional. Decision Making—
When simple decisions become difficult or you let
other people make most of the decisions
you would normally make. ("I can't think right
now, you decide!") When you go to the
grocery store and the clerk asks, "Paper or
plastic?," you can't decide! Letting others always choose
the movie. Depression—Needing more or less sleep
than is usual for you. Withdrawing from friends
and family. Using alcohol or drugs on a
regular basis to feel "normal." We all have
highs and lows, but chronic tiredness or sadness
shows that it is time to seek help.
Here is a list of symptoms to
look for in yourself or to observe in
others for detecting whether burnout is the problem:
complaining of fatigue; feeling overworked; being exhausted; not
sleeping; loss of enthusiasm, energy, drive, team spirit,
cooperation, or optimism; fighting changes; being inflexible, rigid,
or unyielding; being overly stubborn; getting defensive easily;
allowing key relationships to deteriorate; losing friends; becoming
accident prone; experiencing poor recall and memory; rationalizing;
and withdrawing. Take an inventory of yourself and
those around you and see how many of
these symptoms apply. In a very stressful environment,

the entire staff may be showing signs of burnout. There can be a camaraderie of stress and pain. It can become unpopular for any member to do self-care. If one person starts to work shorter hours, take scheduled breaks, or go on earned vacations, the others begin to think of that person as a slacker or not a good team player. It can be difficult to break out of the pattern. However, this type of situation is toxic and will eventually lead to frequent illness and time lost from work, more on-the-job accidents, and lower productivity. If you are in such a situation, you might suggest that the entire group take a stress workshop, or ask whether *you* can. Bring the information back to your coworkers. One person can break the cycle of increasing burnout. At the very least, you will begin to see things differently and take care of yourself. You may need to transfer to another department. If you do, ask questions about how the new department encourages self-care. If they don't, you don't want to go there. Businesses are beginning to understand that healthy workers are an asset. Find an employer who values you and values quality of life. There is no need to let stress turn into burnout.

Enter this reading rate in your drill log and compare it with your earlier scores. Are you reading faster? How is your comprehension? I find that with only a small amount of practice my students usually double their reading rates with the same or better comprehension. If this is not the case for you, do not worry. Keep practicing and you will see results.

Ergonomics and Advanced Reading

Another factor in becoming an advanced reader is creating an effective environment for information processing. Now we will explore techniques for improving your efficiency and reducing the physical and mental problems associated with a poor environment.

An important strategy in controlling the chaos in our work environment is having a physically supportive workstation for our reading activities. Since reading today includes both printed matter and material on a computer screen, I will include information about the most supportive setup of both types of work spaces.

Office ergonomics includes the design of the individual work space, the lighting of the area, the temperature and air quality, the noise level, and anything that adds to or detracts from the functioning of the physical mechanisms of the body. A broader use of the term would include the psychological comfort of the worker as well.

From the point of view of advanced reading, a supportive ergonomic environment includes your desk, chair, lighting, room temperature, and noise level of your surroundings.

Ergonomics for Reading Printed Matter

Desk or table:
- Clear of papers and debris.

- At your natural waist or bellybutton level.

- Book or papers propped up at a 45-degree angle for easy pacing and vision.

Chair:
- Make sure height allows feet to rest flat on the floor.

- Have knees at or above hip level to minimize lower back strain.

- Use a footrest if needed.

Lighting:
- Natural lighting is best; otherwise use diffused, overhead light.

- Avoid overhead fluorescent lighting because of its flickering quality.

- Use a sixty-watt soft white light bulb in a desk lamp to offset glare and flickering of fluorescent lights.

Sound:
- Minimize noise levels whenever possible.

- Play baroque or other style of music set at sixty beats per minute.

Temperature:
- A temperature of 68 to 71 degrees Fahrenheit is ideal. Brainwave activity is at its peak in this temperature range.

Eyeglasses:
- If you wear eyeglasses, use full-frame lenses rather than bifocals for advanced reading. You will want to take in more viewing area with each glance than bifocals allow.

Ergonomics for Your Work Environment

When sitting in front of a computer screen, an ideal ergonomic work space would include the following:

Chair:
- Five-point star base for stability.

- Adjustable backrest that provides lumbar support.

- Adjustable seat pan (height, forward and backward, and tilt angle).

- Edge of seat ends four inches behind the knee.

Floor:

- Adjustable footrest to allow knees to be at or above hip level to relieve lower back strain.

Desk or table:

- Height allows leg room for posture adjustments and distance between keyboard support and knees.

Computer screen:

- Top of the computer screen needs to be slightly below eye level and an arms-length away.

- Keep your screen free of dust.

Keyboard:

- Ideally, is detachable and adjustable to allow for straight (or parallel) hand-forearm posture. (When using a wrist rest to accomplish this, make certain that you do not keep your wrists immobile.)

- Have your mouse or input device at the same level as the keyboard and the same distance from the body.

Lighting:

- Glare on the computer screen needs to be minimized by facing the screen away from light sources or using window shades.

- Use an antiglare screen.

- Avoid lights in the peripheral viewing area.

- Avoid florescent lighting whenever possible.

Posture:

- Head tilted forward 15 degrees or less.

- Elbows supported or kept close to the body.

- Lumbar curve of the back maintained.

- Feet always supported.

- Head and neck upright.

- Shoulders relaxed.

Noise:
- Sound-absorbing wall and ceiling panels minimize noise levels.

- Baroque music played in the background is soothing and supportive for thinking.

Temperature:
- Ideal temperature for thinking is 68 to 71 degrees Fahrenheit.

- Make sure air is well-circulated. Have fresh air, or filtered if necessary, to ensure quality air standards.

Eyeglasses:
- If you wear eyeglasses for reading, you might consider buying a pair of half-strength lenses for computer use. This allows for comfortable focus on the 18- to 26-inch distance of most computer screens. Bi- or trifocal lenses are not as good as full-frame lenses because they have too limited a viewing area, which makes you tilt your head back to see the screen.

Ergonomics of the Hand as a Pacer

When describing the hand as a pacer, I mentioned that it is important to let the arm hang freely from a relaxed shoulder. The wrist is at the same level as the elbow, and the pacing motion across the page comes from the elbow, not the wrist. The wrist is vulnerable to repetitive strain injuries, so it is important for the motion to come from your elbow. Try both motions to see how much more freely your hand moves from your elbow than your wrist. It is important to learn pacing this way, so that you do not need to break a bad habit later on.

Advanced Reading and Your Vision

The eyes are the tools we use for reading, and it is important to understand something about how they work and how to use them in a healthy manner.

There are two major muscle groups that control eye function. The *extraocular* muscles allow the eyes to move from side to side, up and down, and around. We need these muscles to point our eyes in the right direction. The *ciliary* muscles control focus by expanding and contracting the inner lens of the eye. They thicken and thin so that you can see objects up close and far away. In reading, we use both groups of muscles, the ciliary muscles to focus and the extraocular muscles to move our eyes from word to word and line to line.

When we are taught to write, teachers expend much effort in teaching us how to hold our pencil and paper. However, when we are taught to read, nothing is said about how we use our eyes. Children are needing glasses at younger ages and in greater numbers than ever before, and much of the blame goes to the many hours students are expected to read books and stare at computer screens.

The eyes do not naturally focus for long periods of time on stationary objects. The natural function of the eye is to be in constant motion, scanning the world around us, and feeding information to the brain. When we are taught to read, we are told to keep our eyes fixed on the page. We look from word to word and line to line, trying to keep our eyes focused all the time. If you watch someone read, their eyes actually make jerky motions across the page, and they frequently regress.

Advanced reading is much healthier for the eyes for two reasons. Using the hand as a pacer draws the eyes smoothly across the page. Instead of the jerky motion and frequent regressions of reading without a pacer, the eyes flow smoothly, following the pacer. This smooth, constant motion is closer to the natural scanning motion of the eye and is much less tiring for the eye.

In advanced reading, the eyes do not fix on each word in a staring mode that is unnatural for the eyes. The eyes pick out several words at a time, allowing the reader to get greater meaning from each fixation. A fluent advanced reader scans rather then fixes the eyes on any point. With practice, the reader uses a soft focus rather than a hard stare, thereby keeping the eye muscles more relaxed. Advanced reading is more like our natural vision.

Taking an Eye Break

No matter how you read—fast or slow—it is important to take frequent eye breaks. The eyes, as well as other parts of the body, need periodic rest to function well. Imagine how difficult and painful it would be to hold any other muscle contracted for hours at a time. (See sidebar, *Relief from Eyestrain*, earlier in this chapter.)

The following exercise is a simple eye break that you can easily do whether you are at work or at home:

- Sit or stand straight.

- Close your eyes.

- Take several deep, slow breaths.

- Relax your shoulders and do some slow, gentle head rolls.

- Open your eyes and blink gently several times.

- Scan: Look off into the distance, not focusing on any object but letting your eyes wander from object to object.

- Roll your eyes around in circles clockwise five times and counterclockwise five times.

- Drink purified water to keep the body hydrated.

Remember to take an eye break at least every twenty minutes when you are reading. It will prevent eyestrain and help you to avoid needing glasses.

Push-Ups for the Eyes

Like any other muscle in the body, eye muscles benefit from exercise. A few simple exercises done every day will keep your eye muscles toned and working well long after other people begin wearing reading glasses. A simple daily regime would look like this:

Eye Exercise Regime

- *Near-Point, Far-Point Focus*—Hold your hand six inches from your nose and shift your focus back and forth from your hand to the horizon ten times.

- *Binocular rotation*—Roll your eyes around clockwise five times and then counterclockwise five times. Then look as far as you can to the right, then left, then up, then down. Try to focus on your chin, your nose, and then on the center of your forehead. Once this exercise becomes comfortable, you can hold each position for twenty seconds. Holding these fixed positions of the eyes has been shown to increase memory, creativity, and the ability to learn.

You can do these two simple exercises while waiting in traffic, during commercials on television, or at work when you have to wait for any reason. Another simple exercise is to tape a piece of written material on the wall of your office and stand where you can read it easily. Then take a step back and read it again. This time, take a step forward from your original position and read it. With practice, you will be able to read the material from farther and farther away and closer and closer to you. Eventually you will be able to read small print from across the room or when it is right up against your nose.

Baroque Music for Learning

Another tool you can use to increase your focus and concentration, and therefore your ability to read effectively, is to listen to music played at sixty beats per minute. Baroque music recorded at sixty beats per minute is ideal for slowing down the heart rate and brain waves. This type of music helps your mind become sharper and more lucid, and able to synthesize more rapidly. When listening to baroque music, your brain waves slow to six and a half cycles per second, which is the Alpha brain wave state in which you are relaxed and centered. It has been discovered that such music activates and synchronizes the brain waves of both hemispheres of the brain, thereby allowing us to utilize both the rational and intuitive faculties of the brain.[3]

Even if you play the music very softly in your office, and it seems to be covered by other sounds, the music has an effect on your brain. In an office where there is chaotic noise, playing music at sixty beats per minute near your workstation can appreciably lower the stressful effects of the chaotic noise.

Today, almost any music store has a section of music for relaxation and learning. There are modern compositions, numerous renditions of works by baroque composers, and Mozart's music. You can find music for creativity, meditation, learning, relaxing—you name it. I listen to baroque music when I write and find that it increases my mental clarity. Try music in your office and judge the effects for yourself. If you would like to order some of my favorites, see the About the Author section at the back of the book.

Chapter 1 in Review

Stop and think about what you read or learned in Chapter 1 that is interesting or useful to you. We will learn more about memory trees and how to construct them in Chapter 3. For now, using the tree at the beginning of the chapter (Figure 1-1) as a guide, jot down a few key words from Chapter 1 in Figure 1-8 to help you recall what you have learned. You first may want to write down the three main headings from Chapter 1 on the branches of the tree in Figure 1-8. Then, under each branch, add your key words to fill in the details, so that you will anchor the information in your memory.

Figure 1-8.
Chapter 1 in review.

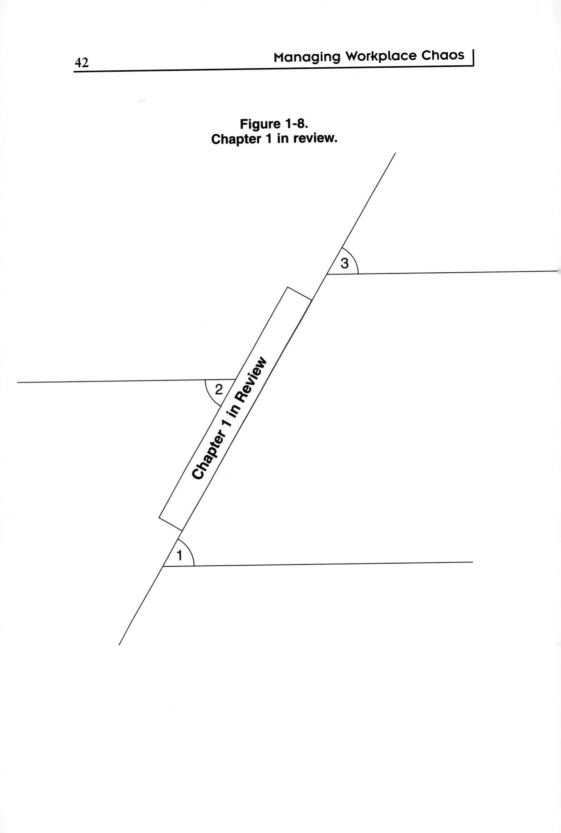

CHAPTER 2

The Importance of Purposeful Reading

Preview Points

- Explore the four stages of comprehension.
- Understand the effectiveness of previewing.
- Learn essential preview techniques.

In Chapter 1, we learned about the physical process of using a pacer to improve how we focus our eyes on the material we are reading. In Chapter 2, we will explore the mental processes of how to improve concentration and develop comprehension.

You will learn how to become a *purposeful* and *flexible* reader by understanding the stages of comprehension we go through to become thoroughly familiar with what we read. Becoming a purposeful reader involves understanding *why* you are reading something. You will learn how to effectively preview, and you will learn that you can decide how much or how little to read.

The number-one key to solid comprehension is purpose—*why* you are reading something and for *what* information. When you know your purpose, you can plan your approach to the

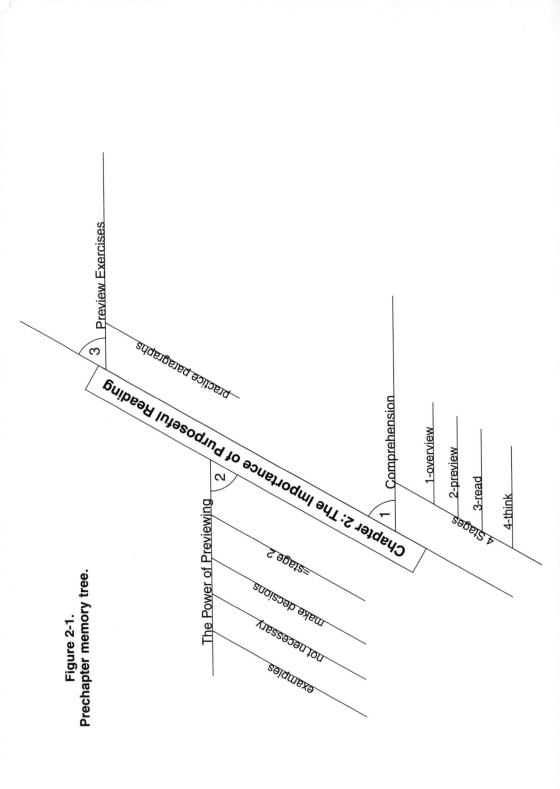

Figure 2-1.
Prechapter memory tree.

Preview Exercises

3

practice paragraphs

Chapter 2: The Importance of Purposeful Reading

Comprehension

1-overview

2-preview

3-read

4-think

4 Stages

1

2

The Power of Previewing

stage 2

make decisions

not necessary

examples

material. The second key is to be flexible by using the appropriate approach each time you read—in other words, breaking the old habit of reading everything the same way. Having a purpose when reading directs the mind to look for information *from* the words instead of merely looking at words. When you know what you are looking for, you recognize it when you see it. If you want to sit and read something from start to finish to enjoy it, great! However, if you need to get through a stack of papers and journals on your desk, you will use a different approach. If you need to gain an in-depth understanding of a topic, you will again adjust your strategy. Becoming a purposeful and flexible reader puts you in control of the information chaos in your work life.

Comprehension

Comprehension is critical to all reading and learning, yet many people have difficulty clearly understanding what they have read or heard. Most of us have never been taught the skills of comprehension, or we have a limited view of what it means. The most common experience of comprehension my students have is from standardized testing in schools. Unfortunately, people usually read for the "stuff they are going to get us on" in tests and quizzes, and they continue to read this way for the rest of their lives. I've met hundreds of people who can test well, yet have difficulty discussing what they read with another person, or putting what they have learned into practice. They lack the ability to form ideas or opinions about reading material because they focus only on names, dates, or other minutia, which has no meaning for discussion. Those facts may be important, but why?

International author and educator Donald H. Weiss, Ph.D., discusses this point in his book, *Improve Your Reading Power.* Weiss states,

> The bad news is that many people reading this book don't read well, don't always understand what they read. And a goodly number won't remember much of it. Don't be sur-

prised. The situation didn't suddenly descend on the continent like a plague of locusts. Americans, historically, haven't been much on reading. Full literacy is only a socioeconomic goal, not a reality. While a large population has consisted of all-out illiterate, a much larger portion has been functionally illiterate: *people unable to understand or retain most of what they read.* The irony in the current collision between the information glut and impoverished reading skills is that few Americans ever could read any information that was in print. Only now, reading is more important than ever before.[1]

And psychologist Peter Russell in *The Brain Book* gives us a clear look at the intention of reading. Russell states, "The word reading comes from the Anglo-Saxon *raedan,* 'to advise oneself.' It does not mean just the ability to interpret the symbols on a page and know the words they form; it is also the ability to advise oneself of the meaning and significance of what is being seen."[2]

As we discussed earlier, the practice most readers have of pronouncing each word subvocally slows them down to a maximum of 400 words per minute. It is not necessary to pronounce each word to understand its meaning. In many studies of the reading process and the nature of linguistics, it has been established that most readers know well over 90 percent of the words.

Words merely stand for things we already know. The larger the group of words we see, the more accurate and complete our comprehension. Because it is difficult to see large groups of words when we read at slow rates, the advantage of faster rates for building comprehension becomes apparent. You never have completely accurate comprehension until you have seen *all* of the words.

The reason you do not make greater use of your visual capacities is because, at each fixation, the eye will take in only what the mind can comprehend. A mind focused on subvocally sounding all words sees only one or two words at a time. The mind is the limiting factor, not the vision, and the mind can be retrained.

As you learn to direct your mind while reading, you will easily be able to respond to larger groups of words.

The Four Stages of Comprehension

Comprehension in reading means understanding what we are reading *as* we read it. The way that we assimilate information is to understand the big picture first. Once we understand the big picture or context, we can then relate the details to the whole, which gives the details meaning. The more we know about a subject, the more we can understand new information.

Think of putting together a jigsaw puzzle. It is possible to put it together by dumping all the pieces on the table and picking them up one by one to see whether they fit. Eventually, all the pieces will fit together—maybe. It makes more sense to first look at the picture to get an overview of the puzzle. Then you open the box, dump the pieces out, and start separating them into categories, perhaps borders pieces, colored pieces, or patterns. This correlates to the preview. Next, you would return to the picture and choose what you want to focus on and proceed to complete that section of the puzzle. You continue this process until all the pieces fit together to form the complete picture.

In somewhat the same way, your ability to build your comprehension and thinking skills will move through four progressive stages of comprehension. You can see how the stages build as represented in the learning pyramid in Figure 2-2. You begin at the bottom with a firm foundation to build on, and progress upward until your purpose is satisfied. The four stages are: overview, preview, reading, and thinking.

STAGE ONE *Overview: Identifying Words, Thoughts, and Phrases*

The skill of stage one is called *overviewing*. Overviewing is conducted by rapidly turning the pages, while trying to identify how the material is organized. The ideal hand motion to use is the open slalom, like a big capital letter *S* being traced down each page. Let your eyes scan the entire page. Overviewing is com-

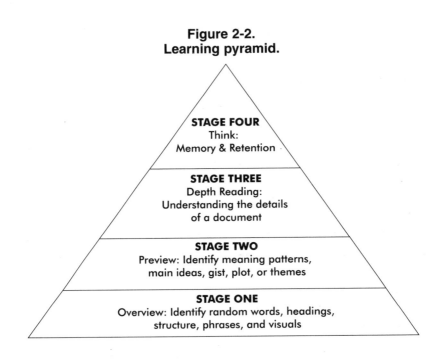

**Figure 2-2.
Learning pyramid.**

STAGE FOUR
Think:
Memory & Retention

STAGE THREE
Depth Reading:
Understanding the details
of a document

STAGE TWO
Preview: Identify meaning patterns,
main ideas, gist, plot, or themes

STAGE ONE
Overview: Identify random words, headings,
structure, phrases, and visuals

pleted at a rate of approximately five to ten seconds per page. Try to avoid counting to yourself, but practice the hand motion on a couple of pages to get the feel of the timing.

When you are overviewing, you are looking at boldface headings; glancing through the table of contents or index; and noticing pictures, graphs, and footnotes. Your eyes pick up random words that begin to give you a feel for the information. Your mind also gets a sense of the location of information, and you have a sense of the big picture. We read with better focus when we have an idea of what to expect. For example, in past reading without an overview, have you found yourself starting to read a document and, after a few pages, thumbing though the rest to see where the section ended or how long it was? This is easily prevented by an overview.

At the completion of an overview, you decide what your *purpose* will be in reading the material (in-depth reading, general reading, or only the gist). After the overview, comprehension is estimated to be anywhere from 10 percent to 30 percent.

This may not sound very high, but remember that it is the foundation on which the rest of your understanding is built. This is also the point at which you can decide whether or not to read the material. A great deal of the material that comes across our desks and into our homes needs no more attention than a quick overview. I know that 90 percent of my incoming mail goes straight to the recycling bin, saving me from hours of wasted time and effort.

STAGE TWO — *Preview: Identifying Meaning Patterns, Main Ideas, Gist, Plot, or Themes*

The skill of stage two is called *previewing*. If you have decided from the overview that the information is something you can use, it is time to preview. To preview means to rapidly survey a text and identify the main thoughts or concepts contained in it. By targeting headings and first sentences of paragraphs while using a medium slalom or *Z* hand motion, you can get a feel for the overall content of the reading material. Remember to use the left-to-right motion to target specific headings and sentences.

Based on your overview and your purpose, your mind will respond to more ideas during stage two. At the completion of a preview, you will have a solid understanding of the key concepts but little detail. The information you have garnered at this point may be all that is necessary for satisfying your purpose. If this is the case, allow yourself to stop there. Comprehension is estimated between 40 percent and 60 percent. This stage is also the goal for comprehension in drilling.

Previewing is a skill used regularly by highly effective readers. Because previewing is a core skill of advanced reading, we will explore previewing in more depth later in this chapter.

STAGE THREE — *Read: Understanding the Details of a Document*

The skill of stage three is called *depth reading*. You read all the words of a document and understand facts, figures, and details as they relate to the main ideas from stage two, and to your purpose in reading the material. The hand motions to use are under-lining or the narrow slalom, covering every line from left to right. When you are finished, you have the ability to write or talk about the information in your own language. Comprehension is esti-mated to be between 60 percent and 80 percent.

You may wonder why you need to go through the two previ-ous stages. Why not just read it? It will take less time, won't it? Actually, you will have greater comprehension and spend less time if you use the stages. In most instances, you will not need to go beyond the preview stage, thus saving yourself hours of read-ing time. You will use stage three, or in-depth reading, only for important documents.

STAGE FOUR *Think: Memory and Retention*

The skill of stage four is *thinking*. At stage four, you become con-fident in your knowledge of the information in a document. You know that you know what it is about. To remember what you have learned, you must spend time thinking about the material. You may go back and review specific sections to anchor your understanding or to gain more depth from the material.

A way to understand this layering process is to think about a movie you have seen more than once. What happened the second time you saw it? You became aware of new things, didn't you? Does this mean that you watched the movie incorrectly the first time? No, it does not. You could focus only on the main plot and characters the first time, but the next time you could pay more attention to the background music and scenery and the nuances of the film. It is the same with reading. You can only absorb so much the first time though. Usually this is sufficient. But when you want more, you can go back with a new focus. Comprehen-sion is more than 80 percent.

Once you completely understand the material, how do you remember it? You remember it by applying a creative thinking process. The process we will explore is called a memory tree. In Chapter 3, you will learn how to construct memory trees for developing your memory and recall skills.

Note that memory and recall can only be developed *after* reading is finished, or in the words of John Locke, seventeenth-century English philosopher, "Reading furnishes the mind only with the materials of knowledge; it is the thinking that makes what we read ours."[3]

By using the four-stage process of the learning pyramid whenever you must read through and sort stacks of paper, e-mail, or Web documents, you will save yourself large quantities of time and greatly improve your comprehension. At first, it may be tempting to skip the overview and preview steps, but these two steps will save you the most time. After you have used the process for a few weeks, it will become automatic, and you will never again feel that you are at the mercy of your information.

The Power of Previewing

Previewing correlates to stage two of the stages of comprehension. A preview is a rapid survey of a text in which you identify main thoughts or concepts. You target headings and first sentences of paragraphs and get a feel for the overall content of the reading material. Previewing a document is one of the most effective skills for advancing your efficiency and understanding.

At first, previewing is not comfortable for some people. If you are accustomed to thinking that you must get *everything* the first time through, you may feel that a preview is too superficial. However, once you understand the stages of comprehension, you will understand that it is rarely possible to get everything from one pass through the material, unless you are a highly developed advanced reader.

Previewing allows the reader to a) determine whether the material is worth further reading, b) plan the appropriate approach and time needed to read it, and c) allow a more thorough understanding of the details while reading.

It is important to remember that we think in concepts, not words. The process of previewing allows our minds to prepare for understanding the concepts of what we are reading.

Previewing is most effective in business and study reading. It is not usually necessary when reading for pleasure. For example, you wouldn't want to know "who done it" in a mystery novel before you even started! But you may wish to look over the book, the cover, and the pages leading up to the first chapter to get a feel for it.

Think of how effectively previewing works for you now. When you go to the movies, you see previews of upcoming attractions. In less than two minutes, you make a firm decision about whether or not to see those movies. And what do you see in a movie preview? You see who the main characters are and who the actors will be. You get a general sense of the plot and time period and you get a feel for the overall tone of the movie. For some movies, you know immediately that you don't want to see them. For others, you can't wait until they are in the theaters. And for some movies, you know right away you'll wait until they are on television or released on video. All this from a short clip! Your mind can do this when you preview text as well.

One mistake I see many people make is to read too much into a preview. When you are done previewing, you want to feel comfortable with the gist only, not all the details. If you find yourself reading out of habit or if your interest in the material draws you to read it all, you must pause and remind yourself to move quickly. If you are going to read it, you will do so later. Previewing is a mental discipline. We tend not to realize how automatic our reading habits are, so initially it is important to focus on previewing. After a while, it becomes automatic.

One of the main benefits participants in my seminars report to me is knowing that they don't have to read all of everything. Once they learn the skill of previewing, they know that it is okay to stop at this stage in a document. If they need more information in the future, they can always go back. I had one participant struggle with this idea until the person next to him pointed out that previewing was better than having everything in a pile marked "to be read," but never looked at. She had a good point.

Preview Exercises

To test the effectiveness of your current previewing skills, read the following paragraphs and jot down what you think the main points are. Following the paragraphs are examples of effective preview answers and answers that would indicate that you may have read too much into the preview. Keep in mind you are looking only for main ideas or the gist of what is presented in each paragraph.

PARAGRAPH ONE

To easily double your reading rate and improve your comprehension and memory, start any reading process by taking a moment to recall what you currently know about that particular subject. This will activate the appropriate "files" in your mind and begin focusing your thoughts for improved comprehension. It will also prevent you from attempting to multitask while reading. Reading well requires complete attention.

PARAGRAPH TWO

In a work situation, we are inhibited—and can even be paralyzed—when a supervisor watches every move we make. Such behavior is a clear message that he or she does not trust us to do the job. The tendency to overcontrol a person or situation often robs the people involved of their initiative and elicits defensive behavior. Although it can be hard to let go, if you have asked someone for assistance, let the person help and get out of the way. Even if the job might not be done *exactly* as you would do it, it is after all being done! If you keep the door open to allow questions, they can seek you out when a step may not be clear. Remember, it is usually the *outcome*, not the *process* that is important. Now you are on your way to effective delegation.

An effective answer for paragraph one would be: *This paragraph tells us to think about what we know about something before we read a book about it.*

Too much information from paragraph one might look like the following: *This paragraph tells us that if we want to improve our reading rate and our understanding, we have to think about what we are going to read before we read. This will help us focus and concentrate. Multitasking is not a good idea . . .*

An effective answer for paragraph two would be: *This paragraph is about effective delegation and how not to be overcontrolling.*

Too much information from paragraph two might look like: *Overcontrolling can be paralyzing, it robs people of their initiative, you need to get out of the way even if the job is not done quite how you would do it, in delegating, the outcome is important rather than way the job is done. . . .*

Notice for the examples of too much information that there is a duplication of the paragraph instead of an interpretation. For some of us, this is a holdover from our training in school, where we needed to remember everything in case we were tested on it. Most of us are out of school now, and we can determine what is important. One thing that is very important is to allow ourselves to become comfortable with the skill of previewing.

Take whatever is on your desk right now and preview it. This is assuming you have already overviewed and discarded all the materials irrelevant to your job. Do not let yourself read no matter how interesting or important a document appears to be. Put those documents in a file to be read when you are finished with your previewing. While you are previewing, make decisions about each document, whether it needs to be filed, passed on, or discarded. Notice how quickly you have cleared your desk. Do this every day and you will never again feel at the mercy of your information!

By using the four stages of comprehension, you gain a tool that allows you to be a purposeful and flexible reader. Combine these mental skills with the physical skill of using your hand as a pacer and you will increase your effectiveness in no time.

Chapter 2 in Review

Stop and think about what you have read and learned in Chapter 2 that is interesting or useful to you. Fill in the diagram of the memory tree in Figure 2-3 with key words that remind you of what you learned. You may first want to write down the three main headings from the chapter on the branches of the tree in Figure 2-3. Then under each branch, add your key words to fill in the details so that you will anchor the information in your memory.

Figure 2-3.
Chapter 2 in Review.

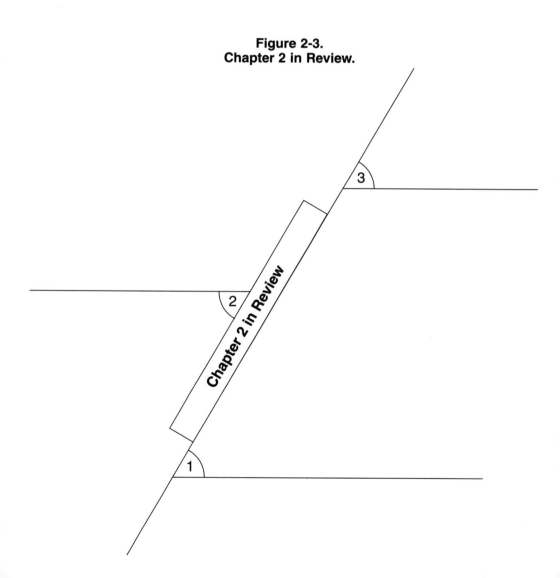

Memory and Recall

Preview Points

- Understand how memory problems develop.
- Differentiate between comprehension, memory, and recall skills.
- Understand the power of thinking.
- Learn the principles of paying attention.
- Learn how to create memory trees.

Memory Problems and Development

"I always forget." "My mind is like a sieve." "I'm having a 'senior' moment." "I can't remember anything." "My memory is gone." How often do you find yourself saying such negative things to yourself about your memory? I hear similar statements all the time from participants in my workshops. Many of us discourage ourselves about our memory or the lack of it, or unfairly compare ourselves to someone who has highly developed mem-

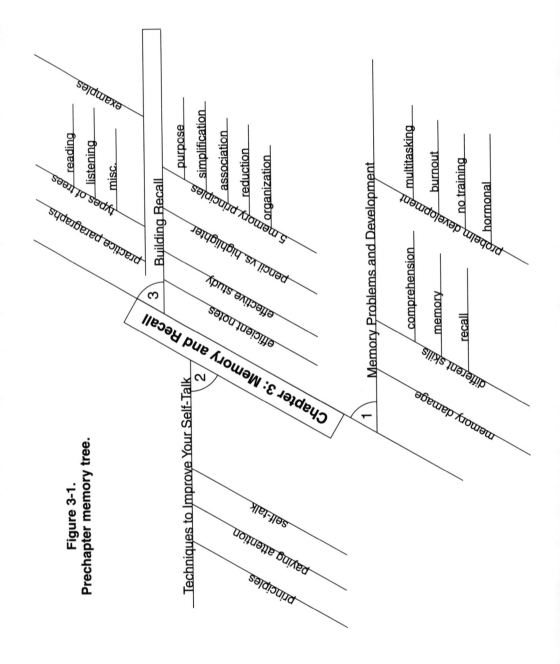

Figure 3-1.
Prechapter memory tree.

ory skills. Unfortunately, this can train us to act as if those negative beliefs are true.

Let's clarify some terms. *Comprehension* means to understand. *Memory* is the storage of information, similar to a file cabinet. *Recall* is the retrieval of information, similar to pulling a file folder from your filing cabinet. As recall relates to reading or listening, it is the ability to think about, talk about, or write about what you have taken in—in your own words. This implies that you have put your own thinking into the making of the memory.

For the most part, we have not learned—or been taught— how our minds work or how to create memory for better recall. For most of us, there is nothing wrong with our memories. They simply need training and exercise. A mind is similar to a muscle. If it has not been used or developed, it becomes ineffective. When you practice and use your memory, it responds and builds, and you will see improvement not only in your recall ability but also in all areas of your thinking.

You have a perfectly good memory. In fact, unless you have suffered damage from illness, accident, birth defect, or severe drug and alcohol abuse, your memory can even improve with time. And for many of us, memory is not the problem, but rather recall on demand.

Let's say you are walking down the street and you run into someone you know. Although you know this person, you cannot remember his name. You may even say something to yourself, such as "I can't remember his name!" and guess what? You can't! You just told yourself that you could not.

We tend to think of this as a memory problem, but it is not. It is a recall problem. Why? More often than not, what happens later on that day? When doing some other task, you will suddenly remember that person's name! The information was in your memory bank, you merely had trouble accessing it at that moment. You needed a trigger to help you remember.

Books and courses teach the skill of remembering. The key is to make an association between a word or picture in your mind and the word or name you are planning to remember. When you want to recall the word or name, you call up the associated image. This practice also ensures that you are paying attention to the person when you meet him or her and are not thinking of something else.

To have good recall requires taking time to create memory. It is not automatic. Many of us get into trouble because we expect to remember what we read simply because we read it. The processes of comprehension, memory, and recall are related, but they develop separately.

How Some Memory Problems Develop

The two main causes of poor recall are lack of training and assuming that memory is automatic. There are also temporary memory problems that we can face at one time or another.

One very common problem today is the tendency to multi-task. Multitasking (doing several things at once, such as talking on the telephone while reading your e-mail and filing) seems like an efficient use of time, but it causes you to be distracted. Chances are you will not remember what was in your mail or what you filed or where you put it. When something is important, we must focus our attention on it. This lets our mind know that it is important and that we want to remember it.

Burnout causes a second common memory problem, which is temporary memory loss. Forgetfulness is a symptom of extreme overwork. When you have a lack of balance in your life and are doing too much, memory can begin to slip. Keeping lists and consciously slowing down can help. I will discuss strategies for dealing with burnout in Part 3.

Finally, a third type of temporary memory problem is hormonal. Books on this subject discuss the short-term memory loss that is possible for women during pregnancy and menopause. Memory problems can be mild or severe. Other than medical treatment, the best suggestions I've read are to be patient, make notes, and not to panic. Memory improves as hormone levels even out.

Techniques to Improve Your Self-Talk

The first step for improving your memory is to improve the way you talk to yourself about your memory. Begin to recognize the types of situations in which you most often criticize yourself. Is it when you misplace objects? When you cannot immediately recall a name? When you cannot remember where you parked your car or what entrance you took into the shopping mall? Or is it when an important detail slips your mind in a meeting?

Whenever you catch yourself saying something negative, pause, delete that thought, and replace it with a positive one. For example, "I can't remember anything!"—pause—"I can remember everything I need to."

Next, see whether you can recognize a pattern in the types of things you forget. Is it a time of day or day of the week? Were you really busy, or were too many people talking to you at once? Once you have a feeling for the situation in which you have memory problems, you are on your way to improving.

We all have the ability to have highly developed memory capacities and recall abilities, but most of us need training. Few of us have photographic recall. A professional speaker who learns the names of fifty or more participants at the start of a seminar and recalls all the names throughout the day has usually worked hard to gain that skill. It is wonderful to see someone have that ability, whether it is an inborn or a learned skill. Unfortunately, we may compare ourselves with that type of person and come up lacking. We all have different levels of ability within the capabilities we all share, memory included. Avoid comparing yourself to someone with extraordinary skills. If you want to obtain that particular skill, you can. But you will have to practice it—sometimes a lot.

The Art and Skill of Paying Attention

The ability to pay attention is the common theme in all memory/recall/learning training. It requires focus and practice. Whether you are listening to someone speak, reading a book, or parking your car, you learn to focus all your attention on what you are doing. You do not let your mind wander to other things.

In school we were told to pay attention, but we were not taught the skill. If one of my teachers had helped me to understand the importance of what I was doing and how to pay attention, it would have been one of the greatest skills that I could have learned in school.

Paying attention is both an art and a skill—an art because it requires desire and commitment, and a skill because it can be learned. Paying attention to another person is one of the greatest gifts you can give him or her. Paying attention to your thoughts is the fastest way to mentally improve yourself.

One aspect of paying attention is recognizing the importance of what you are doing at any given moment. Our mind wanders to other things when we haven't told it what to focus on. Your mind does not have a will of its own—it only does what you direct it to do. If your mind wanders, it is because you have not taught it to focus. This can be challenging when you have many priorities or worries on your mind. However, focusing in the moment is the best thing that you can do during those times.

Paying Attention Principles

Consider the following principles for paying attention while you develop this skill:

- *Paying attention principle one.* If it is important enough for you to spend your time on, it is important enough to focus on. Time is the most valuable resource we have. (This topic is explored in greater detail in Part 2.)

- *Paying attention principle two.* Learn to pause, breathe, and refocus. When you catch your mind wandering, pause, take a couple of deep breaths, and refocus your attention on what you are doing.

- *Paying attention principle three.* Tuning out the world is not rude. When you have honed your ability to pay attention, you will be able to tune out the world around you and focus deeply on anything. Whether it is a person you are conversing with or a project you are working on, you can be completely involved. Athletes refer to this as being in the zone.

Building Recall

Now that we have some perspective on what we call memory problems, I want to introduce information about note taking, principles for creating memory, and the memory tree, which is a tool for recalling information on demand.

Taking Efficient Notes and Studying Effectively

To recall what you have learned in any given situation, you must apply thinking strategies or principles to capture the information. Memory is not automatic. You need to be focused and use skills to create memory, thereby enhancing your ability to recall information.

Pencil Marking vs. Highlighting

When you take notes from text, it may be tempting to highlight things that you think may be important. However, highlighting with a marker actually postpones the learning process. We need to understand that all highlighted material cannot be of equal importance. Out of habit, we tend to highlight a majority of the material in a document. This sends the signal to our mind that we don't have to remember it since we colored it. Highlighting leaves the information in the document.

Instead of highlighting, make a pencil mark in the margin next to information you wish to emphasize. When you have finished with a pass through your material, simply review your marked information and determine what material is the most important. You then record it on a memory tree and erase the mark from the page. The material always stays fresh for your next pass through, allowing you to continue to gain new insight into the material.

Creating memory patterns and using a marking system allows you to efficiently capture the most important information from a document. You can then synthesize and rephrase it in your mind, record it quickly and effectively in an organized fashion, and remember it easily.

Five Principles to Create Memory for Recall Ability

To effectively create memory for recall, you need to implement the following five principles:

1. Purpose

2. Association

3. Simplification

4. Reduction

5. Organization

Purpose

The first principle is purpose. This step actually begins before you start reading. Having a clear purpose tells your mind what to focus on while reading and what to think about after reading is concluded.

Association and Simplification

The next principles are association and simplification. After reading, think about what you have read as it relates to your purpose. What did the words mean? How will you use or apply the information? As you think through these questions, your mind is associating and simplifying what you read into your own language and body of knowledge.

Reduction and Organization

Finally we have the principles of reduction and organization. To begin the process of creating efficient notes, we need to reduce our thoughts into key words and organize them in a visual manner to assist with recall.

Nearly everyone uses this process. For example, when you jot a note to yourself to remind you of something, how many words are on it? Only one or two, right? Enough to remind you of what you already know. Notes do not take the place of understanding or knowing something. Notes are key words that act as a trigger for our memory.

Organization is critical for memory. Some of the memory problems you may be having are a result of multitasking—doing too many things at one time. When you start a task, think of a file opening in your mind for that information. When you are interrupted, another file opens or the information from the interruption is inserted into file number one. Then your phone rings and it is an important customer or client needing to discuss an ongoing project, and yet another file opens up. As you can see, things can start to become mixed up.

Imagine five four-drawer steel filing cabinets lining a wall in your office. You have personally organized all the papers, files, sections, and drawers so that you know where everything is. All of a sudden, there is a freak accident with the air circulation system. All the drawers empty out and papers and files fly all over your office. Fortunately, nothing has blown out of the room. Could you quickly put your hands on the information you need? Probably not. Much like the information in your mind, it may all be there, but if the information isn't organized, it can be difficult or impossible to find. Focusing and organizing your thoughts is a key component for creating memory.

Creating a Memory Tree

For facilitating the five principles and creating effective notes, I would like to show you how successful memory trees can be. Many readers may be familiar with the principles behind memory trees. Similar techniques are called mind mapping, recall patterns, visual outlining, or graphic organizing. I like the term *memory tree* because, to my mind, it builds the way a tree grows. It has a sturdy trunk for anchoring the main points and as many branches as necessary for adding details.

Memory tree structures are patterned logically and spatially. The development of a memory tree is a good disciplinary process because it requires you to logically organize your thoughts and personalize them. It also reinforces your comprehension and creates memory.

A memory tree is a visually organized system of notes. Like all notes, it is a reflection of the learner's thinking about the information. The better organized the notes, the stronger the retrieval will be. Memory trees represent the content, but they do not *reproduce* it. Memory trees reinforce your reading or listening comprehension and create memory.

Memory research has revealed that our brains are neurologically set up with many times more visual receptors than auditory. Therefore, the more strongly visual the information is, the stronger the memory impression. We also know that we remember concepts or main ideas better than random details. And as physicist Albert Einstein and others have noted, our capacity for conceptual thinking appears limitless, while our capacity for facts and details is limited. In other words, concepts will lead us to details, but not vice versa.

The memory tree also allows you to organize the information you have read into a logical pattern of broad categories, which branch out into subheadings of more detailed information, which can be further divided into more sharply delineated facts.

As you may have noticed from the examples in this book, many memory trees begin on the lower right side. Research into creativity and memory processes reveal that we are better at reducing our thoughts and thinking creatively about information when we start at the bottom of the page and work to the top. I have also seen from the participants in my seminars that when they begin at the upper left of the memory tree, they have a tendency to write sentences and paraphrase the original information instead of thinking about it and using key words to represent the information. It may feel awkward at first, but if you try it, you will notice that you think more creatively as a result. In time, you will become efficient and find yourself capturing the meaning more accurately than ever before.

Memory Trees for Reading

First, overview what you are about to read. (Keep in mind this process is best used in nonfiction, personal or professional development reading, or studying textbooks.) Look for introductory information about the author or the topic. Determine the organization of the material—are there chapters or sections? Is it one long document with no breaks? Is there an index, glossary, or other information at the end of it? Are there pictures, graphs, or charts? It is not important to get it all, but rather to get a feel for it.

Next, preview the major divisions in the section of the material you will be reading and begin creating a memory tree based on its topical divisions. When you preview, remember to quickly assess information at a rate that is two to four times faster than your reading rate. During the preview, establish the most important information relevant to your current purpose. Once you find this information, you condense it into key words. It is necessary to understand what you have read to condense it, and this process strengthens your comprehension and retention.

Then read for supporting facts, details, and additional information. Again, condense the new material into key words and add them to the memory tree with connecting lines. It is important to connect everything with these lines so that nothing appears irrelevant. Remember, it is not the purpose of a memory tree to record everything. Instead, record only key information that triggers your memory. See Figure 3-2 for an example based on the previous paragraphs.

Note: **DO NOT** slow down your reading rate to improve recall; when you want to remember something, work on the techniques of comprehension. Good recall is dependent on many other matters beside slower rates. Slowing down is the most inefficient answer to the need for recall. Multiple passes and creative thinking about the relationships of the information are the keys to longer retention.

**Figure 3-2.
Reading memory tree.**

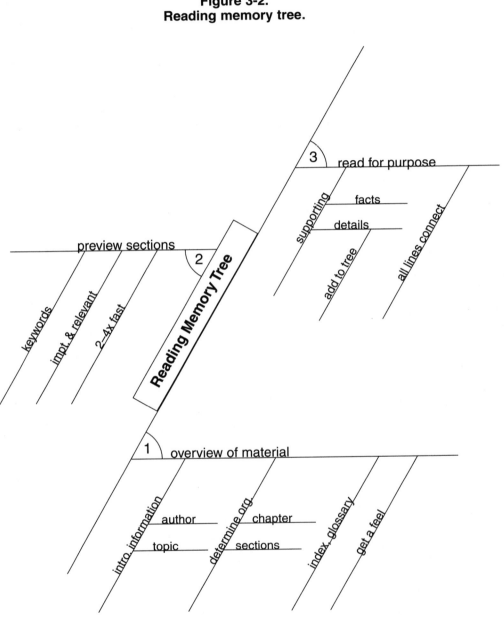

Memory Trees for Listening

A memory tree is a useful tool to help you stay focused and track what someone is saying when you are on the telephone, during a meeting or seminar, or when you are having a conversation with a coworker or client. It can be used in a videoconference, over the Web, or in person.

When someone begins speaking, merely listen. You can think faster than they can talk, so as you listen begin thinking to yourself, "What do they mean?" or "What you're saying is . . ." As you gain insight or information, jot down a few words that remind you of what you have understood. Except for a quote, there is no need to write down every word. Because you have listened carefully and paid attention, the key word will be enough to remind you of what was said.

**Figure 3-3a.
Meeting memory tree.**

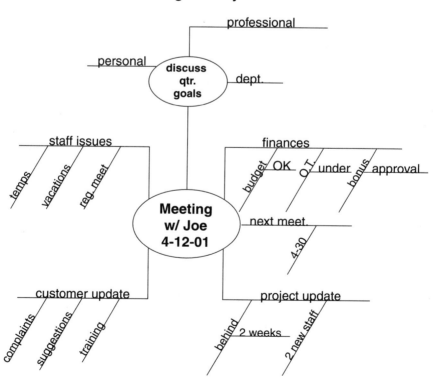

In a large meeting with multiple participants, you can set up the memory tree before the start of the meeting. Base it on the agenda and you are ready to go. As the conversation bounces between people, you keep listening and jotting down key words under the appropriate headings. (See Figure 3-3a, Figure 3-3b, and Figure 3-3c for some examples.)

Figure 3-3b.
Meeting agenda tree.

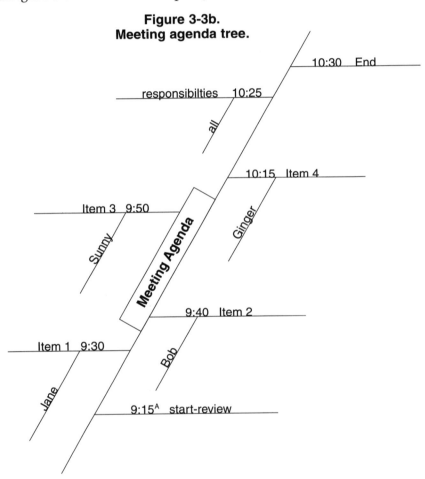

Miscellaneous Memory Trees

Memory trees can be used effectively for many things. Grocery lists (even if you leave it on the kitchen counter, you will be far more

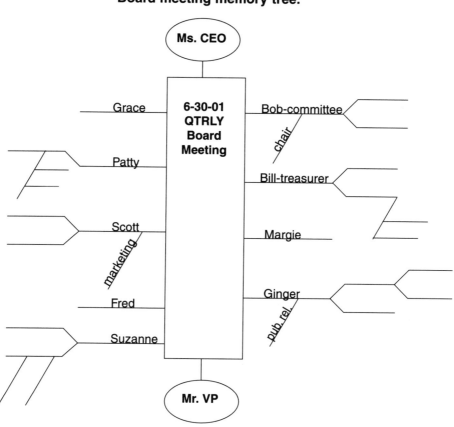

Figure 3-3c.
Board meeting memory tree.

likely to remember all of your list because of the way you created it), family chore trees, directions, and more. (See Figure 3-4.)

Your first attempts at creating memory trees may be brief and incomplete or overwhelmed with details direct from the text or person, but with practice your trees will become sophisticated representations of your thinking. You will learn to select and express main concepts around which you can relate more specific details and ideas.

Remember that it is not the purpose of a memory tree to record everything. Memory trees are only used to record key

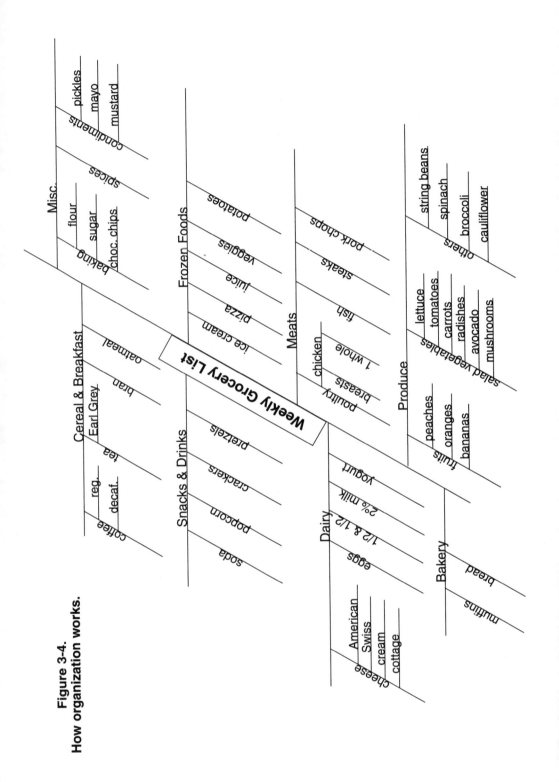

**Figure 3-4.
How organization works.**

Weekly Grocery List

Cereal & Breakfast
- oatmeal
- bran
- Earl Grey
- tea
- reg.
- decaf.
- coffee

Snacks & Drinks
- pretzels
- crackers
- popcorn
- soda

Dairy
- yogurt
- 2% milk
- 1/2 & 1/2
- eggs
- cheese
  - American
  - Swiss
  - cream
  - cottage

Bakery
- bread
- muffins

Produce
- fruits
  - peaches
  - oranges
  - bananas
- salad vegetables
  - lettuce
  - tomatoes
  - carrots
  - radishes
  - avocado
  - mushrooms
- others
  - string beans
  - spinach
  - broccoli
  - cauliflower

Meats
- poultry
  - chicken
    - 1 whole
    - breasts
- fish
- steaks
- pork chops

Frozen Foods
- ice cream
- pizza
- juice
- veggies
- potatoes

Misc.
- baking
  - flour
  - sugar
  - choc. chips
- spices
- condiments
  - pickles
  - mayo
  - mustard

information that will trigger your memory. There are many ways to create your trees.

Try creating memory trees for the following paragraphs and then look at the examples of memory trees for each. How did your memory tree compare? For both examples, notice how few words were used to represent the *meaning* of the paragraph. Keep in mind that to remember the gist of the paragraph, you need only key words, not a duplicate of the paragraph. These examples are not the so-called right way, they are only one way to see each paragraph's meaning. The words you choose need to have meaning for you.

PARAGRAPH ONE

How large is your calendar? Author Danny Cox thinks purchasing a large week-at-a-glance daily planner is a worthwhile investment. He maintains that people who use a month-at-a-glance calendar with itty-bitty, postage-size squares for each day miss time management opportunities. If they write down "pick up laundry" in one of those squares, it looks as if they have a big day planned. Danny Cox believes a larger, more detailed daily planner reveals holes in your day where you can plan more activities. (See Figure 3-5.)

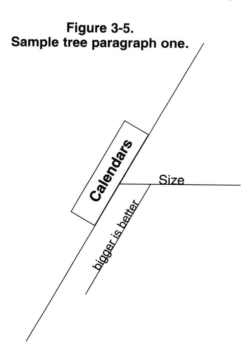

Figure 3-5.
Sample tree paragraph one.

Notice in the example how few words are used to express the readers' understanding of the *meaning* of the paragraph. In my classes, I frequently see detailed memory trees with essentially all the words from the paragraphs drawn on lines, much like diagramming sentences. We are tempted to add words such as Danny Cox, week-at-a-glance, investment, itty-bitty, etc. This habit is leftover from standardized testing in school. If you were in school that is exactly what you would need, but you're an adult at work now. You do not need a word-by-word recall of the information, you need to know what the information *means*.

We are concerned that if we don't write everything down, we won't have enough information. This concern demonstrates a lack of trust in our memory. Remember, key words will trigger the memory of what you need to remember. When I see the example memory tree from this paragraph, I don't think, "Calendar—size—bigger is better." I think, "Oh yeah, that was that information on calendars by Danny Cox. In his opinion, calendars with bigger boxes to write in allow for better time management opportunities in a day."

Look for meaning in the following paragraph and create a memory tree from your understanding. The example of a memory tree in Figure 3-6 utilizes more visual components to assist with recall.

PARAGRAPH TWO

A hook is a statement or an object used specifically to get attention. Hooks are dangled in front of you all the time. You see them on television and billboards and in newspapers and magazines every day. Hooks can allure, tantalize, captivate, and entice you. They are used to get you to buy a product or stay tuned to a television show. (See Figure 3-6.)

Chapter 3 in Review

Stop and think about what you have read and learned in Chapter 3 that is interesting or useful to you. Fill in the diagram of the

Figure 3-6.
Sample tree paragraph two.

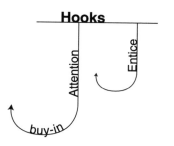

memory tree in Figure 3-7 with key words that remind you of what you learned. You may first want to write down the three main headings from Chapter 3 on the branches of the tree in Figure 3-7. Then under each branch, add your key words to fill in the details so that you can anchor the information in your memory.

Figure 3-7.
Chapter 3 in reveiw.

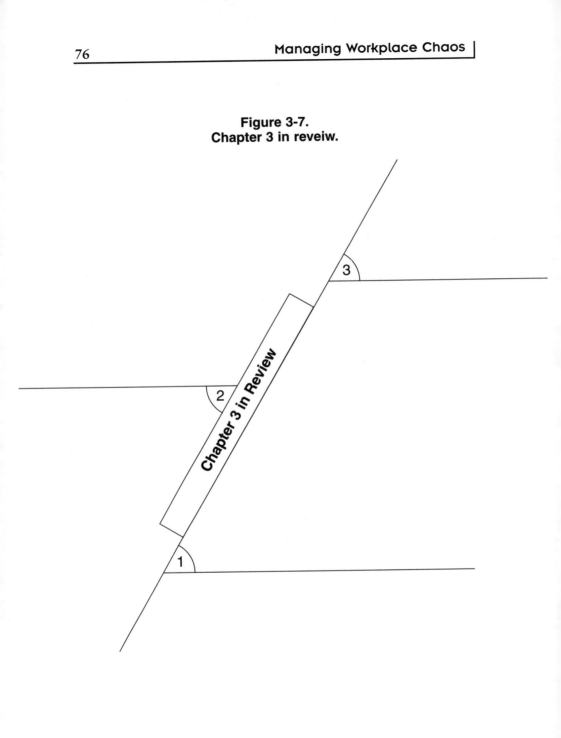

PART TWO
Managing Your Time and Your Information Flow

Time is the most valuable thing you have. Once you have spent it, it is gone. No matter how well or how poorly you use it, time cannot be recaptured.

How do you spend your time? Do you believe that you spend it well? Do you feel rushed or relaxed? Do you feel in control of your time, or do you feel that someone else controls it? How would you like to improve your use of time?

In Part 2, we will explore the principles of time management. We will learn techniques and insights that will help you make the most of the time you have.

I recently heard the term *time famine* being used to describe the feeling of having a lack of time. I think it accurately describes how people feel today. To me it evokes dark, frantic, desperate, and helpless feelings. Are you experiencing time famine?

A Request to the Reader

You may have already heard or read about much of what I have written. I have often found in my seminars that because participants have heard about some of the techniques that I am presenting, they prepare to tune out. Without even trying the techniques, they have decided that they won't work. When you find yourself thinking you know something, pause and ask yourself: "Yes, I have heard of this, *but do I do it?*" A second and similar statement I hear is, "That won't work at my office." Will it *really* not work? Have you tried? Or does it seem too challenging to do? *Time management techniques save you T-I-M-E!* They are worth the awkwardness of putting them into place.

We tend to make excuses when we are uncomfortable facing a challenge or when we feel undervalued at work. It is easier to say that it is "their" fault. I suggest that you give some of these techniques a try. If they don't work for you, you have still learned something. If they do work, you become more effective and productive at your job. It is a win-win situation all around.

Discover *Your* View of Time

Preview Points

- Explore your personal time perspectives.
- Learn to uncover and deal with your *undone*'s.
- Complete a life audit.
- Explore your organization's mission statement.
- Uncover meaning in your job description.
- Utilize effective goal setting skills.
- Learn to create affirmations to support your goals.

The Value of Your Time

You have all the time there is. We all do. We all have twenty-four hours a day, every day we are living. No more, no less.

How do you talk to yourself about time? I sometimes catch myself saying things like, "I don't have enough time." or "There isn't enough time."

Figure 4-1.
Prechapter memory tree.

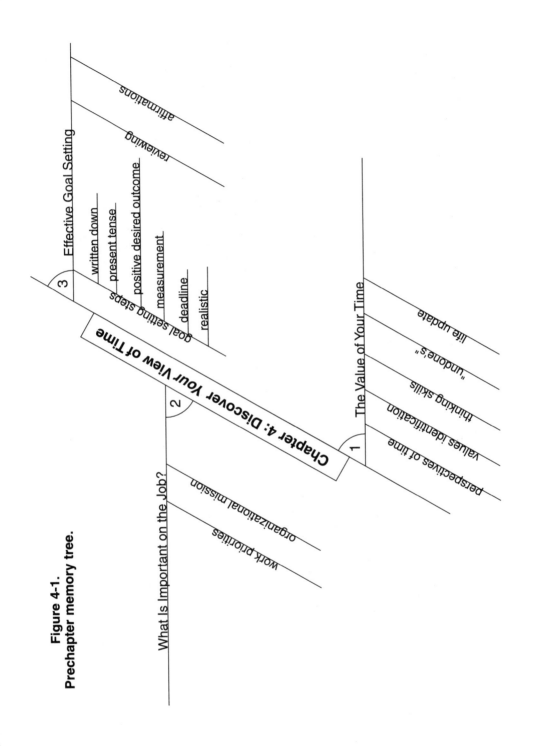

Chapter 4: Discover Your View of Time

1 The Value of Your Time
- perspectives of time
- values identification
- thinking skills
- "undone's"
- life update

2 What Is Important on the Job?
- work priorities
- organizational mission

3 Effective Goal Setting
- goal setting steps
  - written down
  - present tense
  - positive desired outcome
  - measurement
  - deadline
  - realistic
- reviewing
- affirmations

This past fall I found myself saying and thinking, "I have no time in October!" Guess how I began to feel around October 1? You guessed it—rushed and pressured—feeling overwhelmed by what needed to be done. When I finally realized what I was doing, I changed my message to myself. I started saying, "I have all the time there is."

The fact was my October schedule was full. I had seminars scheduled every week, which meant a great deal of planning and travel. In addition, my September and November were full. Overall, having a full schedule is a wonderful thing. It means I have work! But allowing myself to become overwhelmed and stressed-out was taking away from the joy of being successful at my profession.

When I changed my thinking, it allowed me to do a number of things. First, I relaxed and slowed down. Next, I reminded myself of how grateful I was to have these opportunities to teach. And finally, I reprioritized. I had scheduled far too many additional activities along with the work surrounding my seminars for any one human being to complete. I rescheduled some appointments, put some projects on the back burner, and simply let some things go. I found all the time I needed—and more—to get everything done and to enjoy my students and myself in the process.

So, when you are feeling at a loss for time, remember that you have all the time there is. Pause, and refocus on what you *can* do. One way to do this is to understand what your priorities are.

What is most important to you? Do you know? How much of your time do you spend on what is important to you?

One of the values of books and training programs on time management is the opportunity to step back from our lives and take an inventory to gain perspective.

In my Time Perspectives course, we spend the first part of the program exploring our lives to see where we are now and where we have been, and to begin to get a glimpse of where we want to go. I suggest you start your own inventory to gain a clearer idea of where you want to go and what you want to do. Until you know these two things, it is difficult to plan a route to success.

Without a plan, we tend to be pushed and pulled by our environment and circumstances, which leaves us feeling overwhelmed, out of control, and in chaos.

We address the following questions in class. Take time to answer them for yourself. You may wish to use a journal or notebook to keep your thoughts in one place.

The Ideal Day Exercise

This exercise begins with a question, "If I managed my time well, what would an ideal day/week look like?" When you write about an ideal day for this exercise, it needs to be realistic to a certain degree. We are dealing with your life as it is now, not with a fantasy. Start with the first thing you do in the morning. How do you wake up on an ideal day? Are you smiling and full of energy instead of groaning and hitting the snooze button three or four times? Proceed throughout your day, writing about what you would do and how you would handle yourself in *all* situations—positive and negative. After all, you will still run into disagreeable people, traffic, interruptions, and . . . But on an ideal day, how do you deal with it? It may be difficult for you to get started, but I have found that most people love the exercise by the time they are finished. Try it!

When you are finished, read through what you have written and identify two or three things that you would need to change to bring you closer to that ideal day. Could you not take it personally when someone cuts in front of you in traffic? Or, calmly deal with a disagreeable person without reacting to him or her? (You will be amazed how this simple shift can change your whole relationship with that person for the better.) Now begin to implement the changes you identified. Implementing these small changes begins to give you a sense of control over your day, your work, and your life.

How You Want to Be Remembered

This is a great question to help you gain perspective. How *do* you want to be remembered? If, for some unfortunate and unexpected reason you died today, what would people say about you? Would the people closest to you say, "He was really busy and very tired?" For many people I meet in organizations, their mantra both at work and at home is "I am busy and tired." I don't think that is how they would wish to be remembered, yet that is how people consistently experience them. How do others consistently experience you? Is that how you wish to be thought of after you are gone? Knowing how we want to be remembered helps us each day to pause in our business and act in accordance with our values.

Once you have described your ideal day and decided how you want to be remembered, you are well on your way to determining what is important to you and how to manage your time better. Many of my participants find that what they thought was important was not where they were spending their time. Yet, those important things are where you need to spend your time.

Values Identification Exercise

One of the best ways to discover what is important in your life is to complete a values identification exercise.

In this exercise, you list the top ten to fifteen things that are important in your life. Once you write everything down, you prioritize the list and apply a process of paired comparison, which allows you to compare the items against each other. (A complete description of the paired comparison process appears in Chapter 5.)

A man in one of my courses in Argentina was able to work out a major family problem as a result of doing a values identification exercise. The man initially put his family as number one and his career at number four. After completing the exercise, he realized that at this time in his life his career was actually number one. He had unintentionally been paying lip service to his family, saying they were most important and that was why he worked so much. His actions proved otherwise and his family knew it, which caused family difficulties. When he realized his truth, he went home and discussed it with his family. He acknowledged that his career was a top priority right now. He and his family determined how long this would be the case and created a schedule of time that they would spend together. This cleared the air of resentments, and everyone knew where he or she stood. For a completed paired comparison chart similar to this participant's see Figure 4-2.

Figure 4-2.
Values identification exercise.

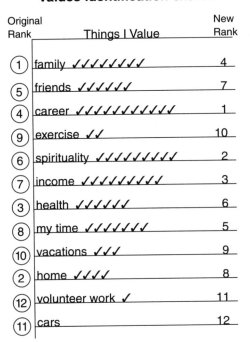

Original Rank	Things I Value	New Rank
①	family ✓✓✓✓✓✓	4
⑤	friends ✓✓✓✓✓	7
④	career ✓✓✓✓✓✓✓✓✓	1
⑨	exercise ✓✓	10
⑥	spirituality ✓✓✓✓✓✓✓	2
⑦	income ✓✓✓✓✓✓✓	3
③	health ✓✓✓✓✓	6
⑧	my time ✓✓✓✓✓✓	5
⑩	vacations ✓✓	9
②	home ✓✓✓	8
⑫	volunteer work ✓	11
⑪	cars	12

Values Checklist

Another way to determine what you value most is to rank a values check list. Review the following list of qualities and pick the ten that you value the most. Then list them in order of priority.

- Accountable
- Achievement
- Adventurous

- Challenge
- Change
- Cleanliness

- Competition
- Control
- Cooperation
- Creativity
- Family
- Financial Security
- Friends
- Fun
- Health
- Helpful
- Honest
- Independent

- Leadership
- Learning
- Love
- Loyalty
- Recognition
- Responsible
- Personal Growth
- Power
- Self-Esteem
- Stability
- Variety
- Wealth

How often have you said to yourself, "Someday I'll do one of those exercises." Make today that someday.

Fine-Tuning Your Thinking

Here is another exercise to help you think through how to change the way you spend your time. Use the following questions to analyze your activities:

- Can I save time without forfeiting results by changing *how often* I do this? If yes, how?

- Can I save time without forfeiting results by changing *the way* I do this? If yes, how?

- Can I save time by delegating? If yes, how and to whom?

- Who controls how I spend most of my day? If not me, can I change this? How?

- What activities can I eliminate?

- When are my most and least productive times of day?

- What percentage of my day is spent on important issues?

Uncovering and Dealing with Your *Undone's*

Undone's are projects, tasks, or chores that you keep putting off or meaning to get to, but never do. They drain our energy and make us feel as if nothing ever gets done or that our to-do list is endless. Examples are junk drawers or closets that need sorting through, that filing cabinet you keep meaning to clean out and reorganize, the pictures that need to get into a photo album, cleaning up your computer software and files, or those thank-you or acknowledgment notes you keep meaning to send. We all have our *undone's*. We need to identify and acknowledge these tasks and put them into a plan for completion or give ourselves permission to let them go. This frees up our mental and physical energy to focus on our priorities.

Start creating a list of things you want to get done. Don't allow yourself to become overwhelmed by the list. This is only a starting point. Now commit to getting two things off the list per month. Keep in mind that projects can be done in increments. They do not have to be done at one time. See how good you feel about getting something done. I know I find great satisfaction in crossing those things off my list. You will too.

A Life Audit

The following list is a collection of life categories with statements related to each category listed under each one. Review each statement and rate yourself using the following scale. Most of us have thought about these issues, but rarely do we feel we have time for them. Yet, in the back of our minds, something is nagging us that we have unfinished business.

The scale:

5 Excellent (I'm completely satisfied in this area.)

4 Above average (I'm doing pretty well in this area.)

3 Average (I'm generally satisfied, but I need to pay more attention.)

2 Below average (I need to set some goals in this area.)

1 Weak (I've fallen behind and need to work in this area.)

PERSONAL AND SPIRITUAL:

_____ I know that I am the most important person in my life.

_____ I have a written mission statement, goals, and action plans.

_____ I have clear values and know what I believe in.

_____ I give myself to others through volunteering.

_____ I set aside time on a regular basis for prayer and/or meditation.

_____ I send myself positive messages.

_____ Total

JOB AND CAREER:

_____ I have refused to settle for a dead-end job.

_____ I continue to develop my talents and skills.

_____ I take advantage of educational opportunities and life-long learning.

_____ I take a proactive position when asked to take on more work and change.

_____ I seek out new, more productive ways to get my work done.

_____ I avoid negative talk about the company and the people I work with.

_____ Total

CREDIBILITY AND TRUST:

_____ I tell the truth. I accurately represent my product, my services, and myself.

_____ I keep my agreements. Others can trust my word when I give it.

____ I give important information to those who need it.
____ I am on time for work, meetings, and appointments.
____ Total

ORGANIZING, SCHEDULING, AND PLANNING:
____ I have a time management system that I follow.
____ I have goals and action plans that keep me up-to-date.
____ I keep my work space organized.
____ I plan time to reorganize and create efficiency regularly.
____ Others are aware of my schedule and know the best times to reach me.
____ I am prepared for meetings and appointments.
____ Total

RELATIONSHIPS AND COMMUNICATION:
____ I express my feelings, needs, and problems with others in a positive way.
____ I resolve conflicts with others in a timely manner.
____ I show appreciation for others.
____ I terminate relationships that are bad for me.
____ I clearly and quickly express myself when I have problems with a coworker.
____ I tell people when I am too busy to speak with them and make appointments.
____ Total

FINANCIAL:
____ I pay my debts in a timely fashion.
____ I have a retirement plan.
____ I have a savings plan.
____ I am satisfied with my income.
____ I only spend within my means.
____ Total

PHYSICAL HEALTH:
____ I am a healthy weight for my body type.
____ I get regular exercise.

_____ I am dealing with bad physical habits (smoking, drinking, overeating).
_____ I listen to my body when I need to rest.
_____ I ask for support when I need it.
_____ Total

Identify two of your lowest scores, either an individual item or an entire group, and write them down. If you have a number of statements rated as a one or two, you may be out of balance in those areas of your life. What, if anything, would you like to do about these issues? Areas that are out of balance can lead to stress, which we will explore in Part 3. For now, just note that the more in balance you are, the more you are able to effectively manage the chaos in your life.

What Is Important on the Job?

The previous exercises may have given you insight into your personal priorities. Now we will take a closer look at your professional life. What are your priorities in your work life? How do your organizational mission, goals, and specific job description help you to prioritize and make decisions at work?

Exploring Your Organization's Mission or Values Statement

What is your organization's mission statement? If you do not know it off the top of your head, go and find a copy of it. Write it down. Think about it. What does it say to you? How does it guide the work you do every day?

Perhaps you do not know. It may only be a group of words to you with no meaning. Or maybe your organization has been working on this statement recently, and you know what it means. In either case, do you allow the statement to help you make decisions and prioritize your days? That is what it was created for.

Depending on your department and the industry you work in, it may or may not be immediately clear how the statement relates to you directly. For example, if you work in accounting and the organization is based on outside customer service, a mission statement that says, "We strive to keep all our customers satisfied with top-of-the-line products and service that goes beyond the ordinary," may not seem to apply to you. You may have to do a bit of thinking or have a discussion with your manager to work out how to use your mission statement as a guide.

All positions in an organization are critical, from the building and maintenance staff to the executive floor. Think of how grateful you are to have a clean and well-functioning building to work in. The staff in charge of these matters contributes to the mission statement by creating a welcoming atmosphere for you to work in. The accounting staff pays invoices and payroll in a timely manner, and accounts receivable ensures that accounts are paid up-to-date. This allows people from other departments to confidently do their jobs. All of this supports the mission statement.

When an organization takes the time to help all employees know how they fit into the big picture, you have a balanced and profitable organization. When this does not occur, interdepartmental wars begin, there is blaming and mistrust between people and departments, and an organization becomes ill. Business visionary Tom Peters in *The Pursuit of Wow!* discusses how he can tell the overall health of an organization and how upper management feels about employees by looking at the state of the rest rooms.[1] I have also found this to be so true.

One of my clients has offices all over the United States and the world. In one office, I found the rest rooms to be lovely. They are clean and bright, and have flowers and toiletries set out for people to use. The people there work hard and feel some stress to keep up with their workload, but overall there is a feeling of well-being and productivity. At a second facility, the rest rooms are institutional. Although they are clean and fairly well lit, they are old and feel cold. The people at this facility consistently talk about being overworked and remark that management does not care what they think. Workers are unwilling to offer suggestions and do not feel that they make a difference. The rest rooms at the third facility are the worst. In addition to being poorly lit, they are dirty and smell bad. Most of the paper dispensers are broken, so the toilet paper is on the floor. There are no hand towels for drying your hands, and the hot water doesn't even have a handle on it. I found that the people there were withdrawn and uncooperative with each other. People commented that they were simply slaves and indicated they believed the company did not value them in any way. There is a constant problem of turnover and people frequently call in sick at that facility.

This company has a very clear mission statement with a values statement to follow it up. Unfortunately, few of the people I met give it serious thought. To them it is merely lip service. Management says it believes in the mission very strongly, yet feels it shouldn't have to take the time to teach others how to put the mission into practice. Talk about a lose-lose situation!

I'm sure there is more to it than the state of the rest rooms, but I think they are a great indicator. What do your organization's restrooms look like? Do they need a little TLC?

How does your organization's mission statement relate to you? For example, let's use the statement, "We strive to keep all our customers satisfied with top-of-the-line products and service that goes beyond the ordinary." If you are in accounting, human resources, or any support-type position, who are your customers? Usually, they are employees from other departments and outside vendors. What is your product? Perhaps it is timely paychecks or accurate invoices. Maybe your product is timely information distribution or appointment calendars kept up-to-date. If you are working in the sales or marketing department, do you know everything you can about your products and competing products? Do you know your customers and how their needs vary? Do you welcome feedback at all times, so you can provide customers with what they need? How do you provide service?

If you work closely with a group or team, it can be valuable to sit down together to explore the mission statement and determine how to use it as a guide for your daily work. Another option is to speak with your manager(s) to get their feedback on the use of the mission statement. If you are a manager, take time to help your department, either as a group or individually. Develop your own mission statement based on the organization's statement.

These statements are critical when chaos is looming. We all need guiding principles to help us make decisions. Otherwise, when we are pressured, we are likely to do what is the most immediate rather than most important—such as sifting through papers or checking voice mail and e-mail instead of working on a tough project. Going through the papers and such can give us a sense of accomplishment, and it needs to be done at some point, but rarely are these activities the ones that produce.

Uncovering Meaning in Your Job Description

In the same way that you looked at your mission statement, explore your job description. Do you have one? How long has it been since it was updated? Does it need to be rewritten?

I have found that people often draw a blank when asked what is most important about their job. Many people are hired to work in a position in which they have previous experience, so they are expected to begin after a brief orientation. The orientation typically covers benefits management, policies and procedures, payroll and taxes, building layout, and emergency plans. The next step is to get to work. A person is given a task then another and another and so on, without a framework to guide decisions in the future.

How do you know what your most important tasks are? Here are some options to help you uncover them. One, ask your department manager. Not as though you don't know what to do, but as a starting point toward becoming more effective. Or two, go back to the mission statement and determine how your daily work supports it. The activities that directly contribute to the mission statement have top priority. Finally, pretend that you are about to go on a long vacation during which you will be out of contact with the office. You have three days to get everything together—reports finished, coworkers filled in, telephone calls returned, and loose ends tied in a neat bundle. What would you do? What can you let go of? You have identified your primary activities.

To stay productive, you must spend nearly all your time on your important tasks. Once you have identified them, you can focus your time and energy there. Once you establish your priorities, it helps you clear a path through the busy work to the work that will give you a feeling of accomplishment at the end of the day.

Effective Goal Setting

Goal setting is one of the most powerful tools for success. Many studies have shown that people who set goals reach them! When highly effective people talk about their success, they usually say that they set clear goals and focused on them. We hear this, and many of us believe it to be true, so why don't *we* regularly set goals?

I know that people are often afraid of failure—or of success—or they fear that they will have to give up something important to achieve the goal. Many people are afraid of setting the wrong goal and getting something they don't really want. Remember, you can always refine your goal to one that suits you better as you start moving along your path. There are also people who resist goal setting because it requires personal responsibility. It can be easier to feel that we are at the mercy of our environment than to make changes. What is your reason?

Most of us have never had a model for the process. Goal setting is not something we are usually taught in school, and only a few of us come by it naturally. If you are lucky enough to know someone who sets goals regularly and sticks to them, he or she can be your mentor in this process.

Many goals create cognitive dissonance, or structural tension. You will be writing and reviewing statements that are written as if they are true, even though they are not yet part of your reality. This tension between what you are affirming and current reality is what your mind works with to help you achieve your goal.

Your mind will look for opportunities to close the gap between what you are affirming and what is real, thereby bringing your goal into alignment.

Six Characteristics of Effective Goals

1. *Written down.* The first characteristic of an effective goal is that it is written down. As long as a goal exists only in our minds, it will always be in the category of "if only and someday." I recommend starting with a blank piece of paper or computer screen and writing (or typing) the word *DRAFT* at the top of the page in large letters. In the beginning, don't worry about the format of how you write your goals; you are merely getting them down on paper. So start listing out everything you want. At this point, you may be general or specific. You goal is to write down everything that you have been intending to accomplish or things you want to obtain (tangible or intangible). Include any dreams you have about what you want your life to be like. The items can be major or minor, but it is important not to censor yourself.

One good exercise I've seen is to keep listing goals or desires until you have listed at least one hundred of them. Since we can often become stuck thinking we don't have desires or goals, this exercise frees up our creative juices. Somewhere—usually between goals sixty and one hundred—a shift occurs. Try it and see what happens for you. The exercise doesn't take much time, and the results can be surprising.

Once you have listed your goals, pick out one or two simple things that you would like to accomplish by the end of next week. We'll work with those first. For example, let's say clean your desk and finish a project proposal.

2. *Present tense.* Write out the goal statement in the present tense, as if it is already occurring. Use present tense verbs such as: (I) have, earn, own, complete, am, write, or communicate. Or you may wish to start your goal statements with the word *My* instead of *I.* It is important to use the present tense, as in " I have a clean desk," rather then the future tense, "I will have a clean desk."

Future tense puts it in the *future* where it may always stay—just out of your reach. Putting something that has not yet happened in the present tense is what causes cognitive dissonance. Your desk may look like a tornado hit it, and yet you are saying, "I have a clean desk." Your mind will get to work on this to close the gap between what you are saying and what your eyes see spread out before them.

3. *Positive desired outcome*. Frequently, goal statements do not follow standard grammatical rules. Again, you want to stay in the present tense. My examples may start like this, "My desk is . . . " and, "I complete the . . ." Both of these are in the present tense and they are *positive*. By positive, I mean I am writing about what *is* not what *isn't*. Avoid writing about what you do not want. If you say, "My desk isn't messy," messy is the picture your mind will focus on. If you say, "My desk is clean," your mind will see a clean desk and try to make what your eyes see agree with it. You want your focus to be on the desired outcome, not the undesired present reality.

4. *Measurement*. Next, whenever possible, include some type of measurement. How will you know when the goal is accomplished? Measurements may or may not be numbers. In the examples used here, I might say, "My desk is clean and organized," and, "I complete the project proposal." *Clean and organized* and *complete* are my measurements. If I had a financial goal, I would have a number such as, "I earn $100,000 on or before mm/dd/yy." The dollar amount is my measurement.

5. *Deadline*. At this point you set deadlines. For your deadline, you state the month, day, and year by which you intend to accomplish the goal. I always include the phrase "on or before" immediately before the date in case I have the opportunity to complete my goal early.

6. *Realistic*. As for being realistic, I do not mean that you won't be able to achieve any goal you set no matter how big. However, you need to look at the commitment it will take on your part.

Great goals require great commitment. Are you ready for it? Is it what you really want? Make sure, too, that the date you set for completion of your goal is realistic.

It is also important that your goal involve only activities you control. A goal that depends on other people requires their cooperation and is a group goal rather than a personal one.

An example I use in my seminars comes from a participant in a course I taught in Australia. His dream was to sail around the world. This did not seem to be an unreasonable goal for him, and so we broke it down into immediate, short-term, mid-term, and long-term goals. Then he told me that not only had he never sailed, he had never been on any kind of boat and did not know how to swim! Still the goal was not unrealistic. However, it was going to take some time. We set a final goal of sailing around to the different ports of the world within ten years. From that point we backed up to the present day.

We ended up with close to one hundred goals. He started with a reality check. He went to Sydney over the weekend to take a short sailing trip around the harbor to see whether he liked it, and he signed up for swimming lessons the week after the seminar. At this point, he could have found out that he did not like water or that he became extremely seasick. If this had happened, it would not have meant that he failed in his goal. Instead, it would have been time to reevaluate. Perhaps what he really wanted was to visit many of the exotic ports of the world and could travel by air or land instead, or it might have been sufficient to watch the sailing races on television. Most important, he would have set a goal and taken steps to realize it, rather than leaving his dream in the category of "I wish" or "Maybe someday."

The outcome is not as important as the process of setting goals. A goal is constantly being refined as we get closer to it and gain more information. If the information we get is that we didn't want it after all, we release it and use the new information we have to set a new goal that fits us better. People who set goals accomplish what they want to in life.

The last time I heard from the man in my seminar in Australia, he was having the time of his life crewing on racing boats, and he had found a new community of friends with whom he could share his passion.

Reviewing Your Goals

Once you set your goal statements, you need to review them constantly by writing them on index cards or printing them out and placing them where you will see your goals regularly—on your bathroom mirror, on your refrigerator, on the dashboard of your car, on the wall next to your computer. The more you see them the better.

Every once in a while, I have a participant in one of my classes who does this. The experiences these participants report are similar. At first, their family and coworkers wonder about these pieces of paper that are posted everywhere. But over time, they begin to ask questions about the process of goal setting—what the person is doing and how. Other people recognize an energetic, happy, and focused person and want the same thing.

Some of you may wish to be cautious about whom you share your goals with in the beginning. Sometimes, there are people in our lives who inadvertently put down our dreams. When we were young, parents or teachers may have thought that squashing our dreams was for "our own good," so that we wouldn't feel hurt or disappointed when we didn't succeed. It is possible that someone in your life might laugh at or ridicule your goals because of envy or insensitivity, or even because of a misguided sense of protecting you from disappointment. You can sense whether this is true for you. If it is, do not share your goals with that person at first.

About two years ago, there was an advertisement on television where people stated their New Year's resolutions, while in the background coworkers and friends laughed and put down the idea. This is not what you need. Over time, it won't bother you if someone does this. However, at the beginning, avoid telling the unsupportive or negative people in your life about your goals.

It can help tremendously to join with other people who are also setting goals. There may be a class or workshop at your community college on goal setting. Such classes and workshops often encourage participants to continue to meet with and support each other after the formal class is finished.

You may be able to find a *mastermind* group in your area. In these groups, people support each other's goals. Members help brainstorm solutions to problems that come up along the way, and they discuss each other's progress toward their goals. There is always a supportive atmosphere. I belong to a mastermind group in my hometown, and we help each other with suggestions and support for getting things done—from cleaning out attics to starting businesses to writing books!

Let's take a final look at the example goals we started with. When complete, they look like this: My desk is clean and organized on or before mm/dd/yy. I complete the draft of the project proposal on or before mm/dd/yy. The final project proposal is complete on or before mm/dd/yy.

Once you get started, you may want to set goals for many areas of your life. If you do, keep the most important and most current drafts of these goals where they are visible throughout the day, and review the remainder once or twice a day. Some areas to think about are your health, career, leisure time, spiritual life, finances, education, social life, community, family, emotional health, and any others that you may think of.

Creating Supportive Affirmations

When setting goals, it is helpful to have affirmations that support what you want and help you to change negative beliefs.

Two areas in which I frequently see people holding negative thoughts about themselves are time issues and weight or body issues. If you want to set a goal in an area where negative beliefs are keeping you stuck where you are, try adding a positive statement about yourself to your goal statements.

For example, let's say you have difficulty being on time. In fact, you regularly state that you are always late. You were even born late! It even appears to be genetic because the whole family is always late. Do you think it would be easy—or even possible—to be on time because of this deeply ingrained belief system? Not likely.

We operate our lives based on our belief systems. Yet, we can change our beliefs at any time. In fact, we have been changing them since we were very young. As we mature and learn more, our beliefs mature. How many of you once believed in the Tooth Fairy? Do you still? Most likely you do not. However, some of our beliefs are so well-ingrained that we do not even notice them, or we think that they are facts rather than beliefs.

Always being late can be such an unconsciously held belief. The way to change it is to first realize that it is a belief, not a fact. You can then set a goal to change that belief. The goal for being on time would be something like, "I am on time for all my commitments on or before mm/dd/yy." Notice that I didn't say, "I will not be late any more." The focus in the second statement is still on being late and is in the future tense. Remember that we use only positive statements and the present tense. The verb *will* will always be in the future.

If your goal statement is, "I am on time for all my commitments," a backup affirmation would be, "I am on time." You write this short statement on small cards and post them everywhere you can think of. Keep in mind it takes anywhere from twenty-one to thirty days to make or break a habit. It takes our mind and body at least this amount of time to become comfortable with the new behavior and for the behavior to become as automatic as the old belief.

When it comes to body issues, many of us set goals to lose weight, but frequently we do not act on them or keep them up. A weight goal would be something like, "I weigh xxx pounds on or before mm/dd/yy." Or you may have an exercise goal, "I walk twenty minutes a day three days a week on or before mm/dd/yy." Whatever your body image goal may be, here is an affirmation that helps everyone, "*I am my perfect body weight.*"

Now, I don't know about you, but when I say that to myself, I hear a little voice in the back of my head saying, "Liar, liar, pants on fire!" But I keep repeating it. This phrase is on my refrigerator and bathroom mirror. Over time, it has helped a great deal. Remember what we said about cognitive dissonance. Our mind wants to close the gap between what we are affirming and what we see in the mirror. Over time, it brings the two into alignment.

I have talked about this phrase in my classes for many years, and have seen some powerful examples of how it works. The most striking example came one day when a woman raised her hand to speak. She had been quiet and attentive but not very interactive until this point in the program. She was a small- to medium-size woman who was about 5 feet 4 inches tall and weighed 140 or so pounds. She shared that at one time she weighed over 290 pounds. She even showed us a picture.

She had tried every diet and medication known, and had had multiple surgeries to staple her stomach. Nothing had worked. She had gone to several clinics and diet farms—again with no lasting success. It wasn't until she went to a local group in a basement of a community college that she began to get better. There were men and women of all sizes, underweight as well as overweight.

On the first night, they were given a piece of paper on which was written the affirmation "I am my perfect body weight." People grumbled their disbelief, but the instructor suggested that this is what they must come to believe about themselves to get the body they wanted. She explained that they had unrealistic visions of themselves that they needed to change before any diet or exercise would last. She told them to go home and stand naked in front of a mirror, look at their entire body and repeat, "I am my perfect body weight." Everyone was to do this every day until the next meeting.

The woman in my class shared that this was no easy task, but at that point she was willing to try anything to get healthy. Over the following weeks, people started to look better. They seemed less dark and anxious or depressed. Many started sharing success stories about actually eating three complete meals (the under-weight folks) or about being able to leave some food on a plate (the overweight folks).

Over time, my participant told us that she started to feel like walking—not exercising, per se, because that would have felt like punishment to her. She said it just felt natural to walk. Then she took up swimming. When she shared the story with us, she was swimming five days a week—again not for exercise, she stated, but because it felt good to do so. To her, exercise always meant punishment. Because of the affirmation, she had gotten to her healthy weight of 140 pounds and had maintained it for five years when I saw her. She said it took a while to see the results, but she consistently felt better about herself and her body.

Affirmations can help you to achieve your goals, and they can help you feel more in control of situations around you in spite of any chaotic environment in which you might find yourself. Two affirmations that I use frequently are: "I have all the time there is" and "All is well right now." These statements prevent me from worrying about future problems that may never happen and remind me to stay focused in the present moment.

Set up affirmations for yourself. Notice how they help you through your days.

Chapter 4 in Review

Stop and think about what you have read and learned in Chapter 4 that is interesting or useful to you. Fill in the diagram of the memory tree in Figure 4-3 with key words that remind you of what you learned. You may first want to write down the three main headings from Chapter 4 on the branches of the tree in Figure 4-3. Then under each branch, add your key words to fill in the details so that you will anchor the information in your memory.

Figure 4-3.
Chapter 4 in review.

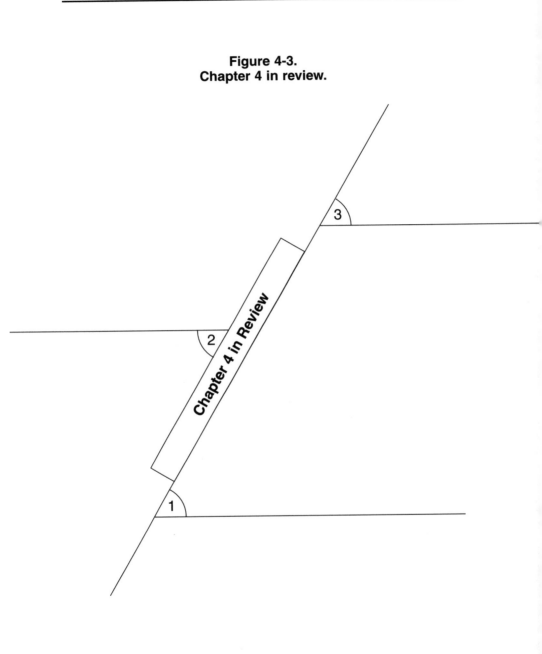

Productivity Skills

Preview Points

■ Learn techniques for dealing with interruptions.

■ Explore delegating skills.

■ Understand some of the control factors for meetings.

■ Learn a new prioritizing technique.

■ Deal with procrastination.

■ Organize your information and space.

In Chapter 5, we will explore skills for dealing effectively with the chaos surrounding our interactions with other people, discuss strategies for dealing with the piles of paper that inundate our desks, and learn techniques for streamlining our space.

People

Working with other people is critical to our success. Yet, those people can often seem to be what is causing chaos in our environment.

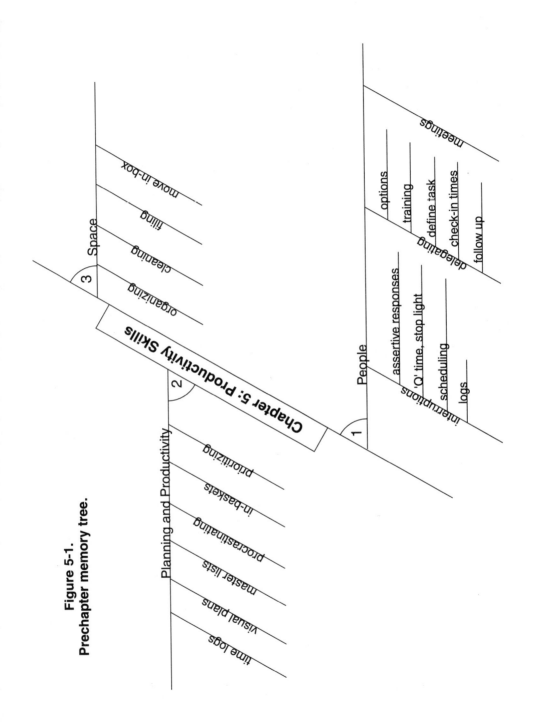

Figure 5-1.
Prechapter memory tree.

Here, we will examine interruptions, the skill of delegating, and meetings. In Chapter 6, we will look at specific communication strategies.

Dealing Appropriately with Interruptions

Most of my participants say that they could get their work done if only they were not being interrupted continually. However, interruptions are a part of most jobs—unless you work alone or telecommute. The underlying cause of most problematic interruptions is the person who allows his or her time to be wasted. We find it difficult to tell others that we are not available.

We often hear that time is money. We have already explored the idea that time—not money—is the most valuable thing we have. We can all find ways to make more money, but we can't make more time. I conduct an experiment in my classes that demonstrates how carefully we spend money, yet how easily we waste time. I ask a number of people in the room for $100. The responses I receive range from "I don't have it" to "Why do you want it?" to a flat, "No." Rarely does anyone have difficulty responding to my request. Yet when we are asked for our *time*, we can't seem to say no. I ask my students to begin to consider spending their time as carefully as they spend their money.

As I write this, I can hear the objections of many of my students echoing in my head, "I couldn't possibly tell someone I was busy," or "We aren't allowed to do that at my company!" When we learn how to respond assertively to interruptions, people do not take offense when we say that we do not have time at that moment.

There are many reasons why people feel they must allow each interruption that occurs during their day. See whether any of the following apply to you:

You don't want to be rude.

You feel you must always be available.

You enjoy socializing.

You like to stay informed about what is going on.

You know most of the answers to people's questions.

You always answer the telephone when it rings.

You know where everything is located.

It is important to distinguish between *necessary* and *unnecessary* interruption. Sometimes we need to allow interruptions, sometimes we do not. All of the previous examples are legitimate reasons to allow oneself to be interrupted. However, we must accept the consequences when interruptions become excessive or begin to diminish our effectiveness.

There are many techniques for minimizing interruptions. Here are some that I have found to be very effective in practice:

Scheduling Quiet or Quality Time

I have seen scheduled quiet or quality time implemented by individuals and by entire departments in an organization. This so-called Q time is simply time when no interruptions are accepted. The telephones are forwarded to voice mail systems so that employees have undisturbed time to focus on important work. The time frame is usually from thirty minutes to one hour. A large Q is posted at the entrance of a department or on individual office doors or cubical entrances. This symbol alerts other people not to interrupt at this time.

In studies conducted by the American Management Association and industry efficiency experts, it has been found that one hour of uninterrupted time is equivalent to four hours of productivity. Many of you are aware of this already. That is why you come in early, work through the lunch hour, or stay late. It is during these off-hour times that you can get your work done.

The concern here is that working through lunch and staying late leads to overwork and eventually to burnout. It also gets us in the habit of not tackling much of our high-productivity work during the day. Instead, we leave ourselves open to more interruptions and allow coworkers to expect us to always be available.

We get into these habits innocently, but they tend to backfire eventually.

Stop-Light System

A similar technique to Q time is the departmental stop-light system. Once again, this is a signal as to your availability for interruptions, but it is more flexible. For this technique, everyone gets three colored pieces of paper—one red, one yellow, and one green—that are about 4 to 6 inches in diameter. When the red dot is posted, it means *do not interrupt,* except for emergencies—such as the building is burning down. The red dot can usually be posted for a maximum of an hour, but I know some organizations that negotiate with employees for different time frames. In some cases, the term *emergency* must be well-defined. Since so many people are now working in crisis management mode, everything seems to be an emergency.

When the yellow dot is posted, it means *proceed with caution.* Think before you interrupt. This is not the time for a social call or FYI update. Only necessary questions and problems during yellow dot time. The yellow dot is typically up most of the day, thereby reminding coworkers not to interrupt frivolously.

When the green dot is displayed, it is open season. *Anything goes.* The doctor is in. During these times, you are perhaps organizing files, straightening your office, or doing general paperwork. Green dot time usually lasts up to fifteen minutes.

The most important factor of this system is that it helps people to think before they act. We can all get so caught up in what we are doing that we interrupt someone without thinking. We do not do this purposefully, and neither do most of the people who interrupt us. The stop-light system allows us to value our own time and that of others.

Assertive Responses to Interruptions

Another key for minimizing interruptions is to pay attention to your automatic responses when you are interrupted. What do you say when someone drops in? Ideally, you look at the person with a smile on your face and say, "Hi George, good to see you. I'd love to talk with you but I'm in the middle of this project. Could we catch up at 3:15 this afternoon?" George will not be offended. You have shown him that you're glad to see him and told him when you can talk. If he has a quick question, he will ask it and be gone. However, he will not think it is the proper time for chatting with you.

In learning how to use an assertive response, it is important to focus on the person and be pleasant. The intention behind your words is critical. When we are deeply focused on our work, we tend to have a wrinkled forehead and a pinched look on our faces. We are usually not aware of this look, so that when a person interrupts us, we keep the "cross" expression on our faces as we look up. We mean no harm by the look, yet the receiver thinks it is directed at him or her.

Looking cross and mean is one way of getting people to avoid you, but that is usually not our goal. If we greet the interrupter pleasantly, and say that although we are glad to see him or her, we are busy now and must set a time to meet later, we have forestalled the interruption and kept a friendly association with our coworker.

On the other side of the issue, when you need to interrupt someone, being assertive can help, too. When you need to speak with someone, do him or her a courtesy. Stop, knock, pause, and pleasantly and clearly say, " Hi Ginger, I need to speak with you about project X. I think it will take us twenty minutes. When will be a good time for you?" More often than not, Ginger will make time at that moment for you. She knows you have a specific purpose and have thought out what you need to say. Or, she has the option of making an appointment with you later in the day. If she looked cross when you opened the door, chances are she is smiling when you leave because of the courtesy you showed her.

Scheduling Interruption Time

Whenever possible, schedule your meetings and telephone calls with others and also let them know when you are available to receive telephone calls and meet with people in the office. When someone has a scheduled meeting with you or knows when you are available, he or she will be more likely to use that time block than to interrupt you at an inconvenient time.

I have seen a client take these suggestions I have made and combine them in a very useful manner. Each person in the office has a small white board posted on his or her office door or cubical. There is a section for the red, yellow, and green dots and a daily timetable. The timetable indicates when the individual is available and when he or she is not. People can sign up for time in the available slots. My client reports that everyone in the office feels a greater sense of control over their time and a security in knowing when they are available to each other.

Creating an Interruption Log

One final technique you may wish to try is an interruption log in which you record your interruptions. When you are uncertain where in your day, or how often, or why you are being interrupted, a log can help. This log is for your use only, it is not to be utilized to criticize another person. You create a time line down the left hand side of a sheet of paper, and across the top of the paper you have slots for the names or initials of the people or situations that interrupt your day. (See Figure 5-2.) Immediately after the interruption, place a check or draw a line to indicate the time taken and perhaps to jot a note to yourself as to what it was about. Do this a couple days a week for a few weeks until you see a pattern.

Next, examine the logs. Are there certain times of the day or days of the week that have more frequent interruptions? Why? Could they be eliminated with updates via e-mail, voice mail, or a meeting? Are there certain people who interrupt more often? Why? Are they asking legitimate questions? Do they need more access to information you have? Do they need training? Or are they simply socializing?

In Figure 5-2, we have interruptions from Joe, Mary, telephone, pager, Allen, and M.J. Joe and M.J are not a real problem. Mary had a personal issue, which took up a good portion of the

Figure 5-2.	
Interruption log.	

Time	Joe	Mary	phone	pager	Allen	M.J.
8:00			✓		│	
8:15			✓		│	
8:30			✓	✓	│	
8:45			✓	✓	│	
9:00	│		✓	✓		
9:15	│			✓		
9:30	│		✓	✓		
9:45	│	│				│
10:00	│	│	✓			│
10:15		│	✓	✓	│	│
10:30					│	│
10:45			✓			│
11:00			✓			
11:15			✓			
11:30			✓			
11:45			✓	✓		
12:00				✓	│	
12:15				✓	│	
12:30			✓			
12:45		│		✓		
1:00		│		✓		
1:15		│	✓			
1:30		│	✓		│	
1:45		│			│	
2:00		│	✓		│	
2:15		│	✓			│
2:30		↓	✓			│
2:45						│
3:00			✓		│	│
3:15			✓	✓	│	
3:30				✓		
3:45			✓	✓		
4:00	│			✓		
4:15	│		✓	✓	│	
4:30			✓		│	
4:45			✓			
5:00						

afternoon. Is this a habit with Mary or a one-time occurrence? If it happens all the time, something needs to be done about it because it is significantly interfering with your work. Allen is interrupting far too often. He either needs training, more information to do his job, or is socializing too much. The telephone and pager columns indicate how often we answered calls. We might use this information to determine when to forward calls to our voice mail system. With so many interruptions, it is no wonder we can't get any work done.

Seeing the pattern of your interruptions, and recognizing some of the causes, gives you the information you need to make changes. You can now be proactive instead of reactive. Author Alec Mackenzie in *The Time Trap* states, "So you see that old devil, human nature, has let you into two traps: Because of ego, or other traits, you accept phone calls and allow yourself to be interrupted, and then you place blame for the interruption on the person who placed the call."[1]

With these tools, you can begin taking charge of your interruptions and therefore your time. Having a sense that you control your use of time will go a long way toward eliminating the chaos in your workday.

A Different View of Delegating

In my seminars and coaching sessions, I frequently hear complaints about delegating. From the delegators, I hear complaints about incomplete and unsatisfactory work. They often feel they have to do the work over again themselves so that it is done correctly. From the delegatees, I hear how they feel dumped on. They are tossed a file, given little or no instruction, and asked to complete a task they have never done before, or have done only parts of. They feel frustrated, confused, and eventually resentful when they are blamed for incomplete work.

My definition of delegating is that it is a training, mentoring, esteem-building process. To perform well, people need to know what they are expected to do. They need to know how thoroughly they need to do it, what resources and authority they have and, when they have completed a task, how well they did it. If you are on the receiving end of delegation, make certain that these steps have been attended to.

Delegation takes commitment in people, time, and resources. The payoffs are great, but the groundwork must be done first.

Taking on more and more work for whatever reason, eventually leads to overwork, communication problems, and burnout. We will discuss the symptoms and stages of burnout in Part 3. Meanwhile, learning how to delegate will take you a long way toward avoiding burnout.

The first step in delegation is finding someone to delegate to. If you are a manager and have an adequate staff, the answer is obvious. If not, you may be able to find a staff member or coworker who is looking for more responsibility. You can delegate tasks to him or her, or possibly share tasks. In addition, your manager can be a resource for you by speaking with his or her peers to determine whether there is a staff member who could be cross-trained on one or two of your routine tasks.

If you are fortunate enough to find such an individual, knowing the rules of delegating is the most critical element for getting the task done successfully the first time. Remember, failure of the assigned task is usually the fault of the person who delegated the task in the first place, not the person who attempted to complete the task.

If you do not have anyone to delegate to, you are probably a delegatee. The following steps may be useful to you as a guideline for asking questions before—and gaining clarification during—your attempts to complete a task that has been delegated to you.

Consider the following five-step approach to delegating tasks for successful results:

1. *Consider your delegation options.* Who would be a good candidate for the task? Is there more than one person you could consider? Talk with them about the possibility of being given the task to see how receptive they are. Discuss the necessary time commitments.

2. *Think through all the possible training needs.* If the person you plan to delegate to tends to be rushed for time, he or she may need time management training first. You may need to assist this person in planning and scheduling his or her workflow to accommodate the new work. If the task requires knowledge of computer software or business functions outside his or her normal work, you need to set up training and give the person time to feel more comfortable with the new skills before starting on the delegated task.

3. *Clearly define the task.* What are the core objectives and optimum results expected? Discuss the importance and value of the task and how it contributes to the mission of the department or organization as well as to the person's own career development. Finally, clearly state his or her scope of responsibility and level of authority. When necessary, ensure that you inform other persons or departments of your delegatee's new position and authority, so that they are prepared to cooperate with him or her. You do not want your delegatee facing unnecessary resentments or roadblocks. Ensure that his or her path is clear.

4. *Schedule check-in times and communicate best times for quick questions.* Depending on the delegatee's level of experience and learning methods, you will need to schedule more or less time to get together to check progress and provide needed assistance. This prevents any surprises from occurring when it is too late to fix them. It is also important for the delegatee to know when it is permissible for him or her to interrupt you to ask questions. Let the delegatee know the best times for speaking with you.

5. *Follow-up.* Spend a scheduled amount of time together to discuss the process and the outcomes of the project. At this time, you can ask for and give feedback. First, *ask* the delgatee what he or she felt successful at in completing the task. Be sure to allow only successes. Many people are so accustomed to being told what they did wrong that they will focus only on what they didn't accomplish. Refocus them on the positive. When the delegatee is finished, you tell him or her what *you* think went well. Again, be positive only.

Next, *ask* the delegatee what he or she would do differently next time. Hindsight is always 20/20. We learn best from experience. Even though you may be discussing mistakes, frame them in the positive context of how to improve next time. For example, knowing what they know now, what will they change?

When the delegatee is finished, you may or may not have something to add. If you do, *it is critical to keep your suggestions positive*. Phrase them as follows: "This is what I would do (or have done) when faced with a similar problem."

An example of step five might sound like this:
Anna is the delegator and Will is the delegatee.

> **ANNA:** Congratulations Will, the new filing system is in place. Let's take some time and discuss the project to determine where you go from here. First, tell me what you felt you did well. What were your successes?

> **WILL:** Thanks again for coaching me through this Anna. One of the things I think went really well was the splitting up of paper and electronic systems. With the size of our department, the old system of trying to combine everything wouldn't have worked. I just wish . . .

> **ANNA:** Hold on, Will. Only successes, OK?

> **WILL:** OK. Well, other than that, I guess I feel good about keeping mostly to our schedule and finishing on time for the board meeting.

> **ANNA:** That's great, Will. I also see all these things as successes. But I also noticed how you researched other departments and outside

resources to get ideas on how to best manage our growing files, as well as keeping future growth in mind. I hadn't thought of that. Thanks to you, we won't need to redo this again for quite some time. Your system is flexible and can grow and change with us!

WILL: Thanks, I didn't think it was that big of a deal.

ANNA: It was to me and I mentioned your process to my boss. She may be interested in having you consult with other departments on your system. Now, let's talk about what you might do differently next time. Knowing what you know now, what would you change?

WILL: One of the things I would definitely do next time is talk with a few more people first to see what problems they were having. I would also have given myself more time on the trial runs with the new software and more training time with the computer support group.

ANNA: Those all sound like good ideas to implement if this needs to be carried over to other departments. One thing I'd have done is use more of my available resources.

WILL: What do you mean?

ANNA: Things like asking more questions and not feeling as though you need to do all this by yourself. I know the first couple times I was on a task on my own, I didn't ask any questions. I felt I was supposed to know it all, when I didn't. I got really frustrated until my manager let me know that I wasn't expected to know everything and that it was OK to ask questions.

WILL: Wow, it's great to hear that. I would have liked to work more closely with you, but I didn't want to waste your time.

ANNA: It is not a waste of my time to help you succeed. Let's make sure we more clearly discuss my available times in the future. I want you to feel you can come to me with questions.

WILL: OK. Great. Is that all?

ANNA: Why don't you review what we have discussed so I can make sure I covered everything I intended to and that we clearly understand each other.

In a process like this one, everyone walks out feeling successful. Sometimes these conversations are more difficult than others, but the time spent is well worth it. It can be easy to skip this step in the chaos of everyday work, but it is a critical step for success.

Finally, review what has been discussed and have the delegatee repeat the next step he or she is to take. If the task is to be done again, have the delegatee outline a plan of action and return to step three. Ultimately, you want the person to move from dependence on you to complete independence on this particular task.

Merrill Douglass captures the value of delegating in his book *ABC Time Tips*. "Delegate as often as you can . . . it gains time, increases motivation and builds people."[2] This is exactly what many businesses need today for managing their chaotic environments.

Meetings, Meetings, Meetings

My favorite quote in reference to meetings is from Herbert Prochnow, who said, "A committee of three often gets more done if two don't show up."[3]

Meetings are one of the biggest time and money wasters in organizations today. Even worse, I have seen them become huge *demotivators* in companies both large and small. Unnecessary meetings are among the top complaints of people today at all levels in an organization. Administrative professionals complain that they are asked to take meeting notes (that almost nobody reads) on topics they are the least qualified to understand merely because "it has always been done that way." Then there are the individuals who don't know why they are there and, finally, the two or three people who have an issue and actually want to be there, but whose issue never makes it to the table.

Meetings can be effective, but like many other things, they take effective planning and a commitment to agreed-upon ground rules.

First, determine whether you really need to have this meeting. One way to begin is to find out why the meeting was established in the first place. Frequently, when I ask this question, someone will say, "We've always had a Monday morning meeting." My next question is, "Do you *need* a Monday morning meeting?" Often the answer is no. If any meeting at all is needed, it is not on Monday.

Another option is to have meeting attendees fill out a questionnaire on meeting performance. This needs to be done anonymously. Ask questions like: Was the meeting necessary? Is there a clear purpose for the meeting? Did you feel you needed to attend? Did everyone participate? Was everyone prepared and on time? Did it end on time? Was the meeting well-organized? Was the meeting worth what it cost in time, money, and morale? The answers to these questions can give you a good start on eliminating ineffective meetings or making the changes necessary to hold effective meetings.

The following are a few good reasons for holding a meeting:

■ Clarifying departmental or team goals

■ Giving and receiving feedback on ongoing operations and projects

■ Having a group discussion of ideas

■ Solving problems

■ Sharing information with a large group

■ Getting immediate reactions to new projects, policies, or procedures

■ Fulfilling a legal requirement

■ Reconciling conflict among members

It is *not* a good idea to have meetings that are unnecessary (to the majority of the group), meetings that involve one-way communication (you can do this in a memorandum), or meetings that people attend merely for courtesy sake or for "face" time (they don't really need to be there, but they come because they want the boss to see their face).

Try the following techniques for more successful meetings:

■ The smaller the meeting the better—no more than five to nine people.

■ Establish agreed-upon ground rules, such as start and end on time—no exceptions!, no revisiting closed subjects, no sidebar conversations, no interruptions.

■ Implement a facilitation rotation—each member takes turns running the meeting and keeping everyone to the agreed-upon ground rules. You set up a rotation so that every member will have this responsibility.

■ Make sure you distribute a detailed agenda that includes the time limits of the meeting, names of people responsible for different topics, a summary of each topic, and a time limit for each topic.

■ Everyone takes their own notes, or a scribe is designated for each meeting to take notes where everyone can see them—for example, on a white board that prints out, a flip chart, or a laptop hooked up to a large screen in the room.

People only complain about ineffective meetings. They generally enjoy the productive ones, because sharing information allows them to work more efficiently.

Most people I work with want to do something effective with their meetings but don't know how. Many feel they have no control over the meetings they attend. It is ironic that all organizations need productive meetings, yet few do anything to teach employees the necessary skills. And then there are the companies where training is provided, there are signs on the wall with the ground rules, yet no one ever follows them (usually because leadership does not model the behavior). You can lead a horse to water . . .

Of the many issues that create chaos for people, meetings can be one of the easiest to solve. But it takes teamwork, communication, and commitment.

Planning and Productivity

Knowing what to do, and in what order to do it, is a key skill for managing chaos. Learning to effectively prioritize will keep you on track with your goals.

The traditional process of prioritizing usually has you list items using the ABC system. Letter *A* is for high-priority items, letter *B* for medium priority, and letter *C* for low priority. When additional categorization is needed, this method uses the numbers one, two, and three to further designate priority. I have met a few people for whom this system works. However, it is ineffective for most people. They find that they can end up having more than twenty A1 priority items and feel that they are right back where they began.

A process I teach in time management training that goes beyond the ABCs and 123s is called paired comparison. This process allows you to consider everything you need and want to do and compare it to everything else. You are able to take into account deadlines and length of time, as well as the relative importance of each task.

To begin using the paired comparison process, you list all the items you want to accomplish within a certain time frame, such as a week or day. Don't worry about order or priority right now.

Once you have everything listed, compare your first item with item number two (only consider these two items) and ask yourself, "If I could do only one of these, which one would I do?" Place a check mark next to the item you choose. Now compare your item number one with item number three on your list (again consider only the first and third items). Ask yourself the question again, and place a check mark next to the item you choose. Continue this process with number one and number four, and so on. Once you have finished, you will have independently compared your first item to all the others on your list. You are done with the first item for now. Next, compare your second item to your third (only consider these two) then two to four and so on, placing a check mark next to the one you choose each time. When you are finished with item number two, move to number three and compare it to all the remaining items on your list. Continue the process, moving down your list, comparing two items at a time. When you are completely done with the entire list, the item with the most check marks next to it is your top priority. If you have the same number of check marks next to more than one item, pair them against each other to establish the priority order.

The following table is an example of what the process would look like:

Items to be done:
A) Sort mail, e-mail, and faxes. . . . . ✓✓
B) Complete draft outline for Chapter 6. . . . . ✓
C) Prepare and mail invoices. . . . . ✓
D) Work on Schedule C of tax return.
E) Organize office.
F) Pay bills. . . . . ✓
G) Prepare bank deposit. . . . . ✓

Once I have listed the items, I begin the process of comparing them. I start with comparing item A to B, then A to C, A to D, A to E, A to F, and A to G. I place a check mark next to one item each time I make a choice. When I finish, it looks like the previous example.

Now I proceed to comparing item B to C, B to D, B to E, B to F, and B to G. When I finish it looks like the following:

Items to be done:
A) Sort mail, e-mail, and faxes............✓✓
B) Complete draft outline for Chapter 6.....✓✓✓
C) Prepare and mail invoices. ....✓✓
D) Work on Schedule C of tax return.
E) Organize office.
F) Pay bills............................✓✓
G) Prepare bank deposit..................✓✓

Now I move to item C. I compare C to D, C to E, C to F, and C to G. Now it looks like this:

Items to be done:
A) Sort mail, e-mail, and faxes............✓✓
B) Complete draft outline for Chapter 6.....✓✓✓
C) Prepare and mail invoices ....✓✓✓✓✓
D) Work on Schedule C of tax return.
E) Organize office.
F) Pay bills............................✓✓
G) Prepare bank deposit..................✓✓

When I have completed the comparison process, my list looks like the following:

Items to be done:
A) Sort mail, e-mail, and faxes............✓✓
B) Complete draft outline for Chapter 6.....✓✓✓
C) Prepare and mail invoices..........✓✓✓✓✓
D) Work on Schedule C of tax return..........✓
E) Organize office.
F) Pay bills. ....✓✓✓
G) Prepare bank deposit. ....✓✓✓✓

My first priority is to work on item C, which is to prepare and mail my invoices. Next is item G (prepare the bank deposit), then F (pay bills), then B (work on outline), then A (sort the mail), then D (work on tax return), and finally E (organize the office). I work on the items in this order or plot them out on a visual schedule throughout a week.

With the items prioritized, there is never a question as to which item I need to do first. Instead of feeling swamped by many priority items, I work on number one and proceed from there. This saves me time and, even more, it saves all that energy I might have expended in trying to decide what to do.

Prioritizing Your In-Basket (Paper and Electronic)

We cannot give equal time to everything that comes into our office. We have to prioritize. A message from a coworker can be more important than a message from our boss, if it involves a time constraint. A project you are working on together could be stalled if you don't answer the e-mail.

Here are some questions to ask yourself to help you to decide what to read and what to get rid of:

- Who wants me to know?

- Is it *really* important?

- Is it something I need immediately?

- What would happen if I didn't read it or didn't read it now?

  More questions to try:
- What depends on my reading this now?

- What else will *not* happen if I don't read this?

- If I don't read this, will I or someone else be able to do other things?

- How would not reading this affect other people or processes?

How you answer these questions will tell you what to read first and when. The answers will supply an organizational framework for your reading and explain why you are reading things in a given order. Also, keep in mind that want-to-know reading takes a back seat to need-to-know items. To gain control over your reading habits, learn to distinguish between what you need to know to get your job done, what you'd like to know because of your interest, and what can be immediately discarded.

Beating Procrastination

Procrastination creates chaos. When you put off doing important or difficult tasks to do seemingly "urgent" ones, other tasks keep piling up until you don't know where or how to get anything done.

Why do you procrastinate? Sometimes we all have a problem getting started, yet postponing the things we know we need to do creates a number of problems—for ourselves, our coworkers, and our organizations. When we don't want to do something, we tend to dither around with minor tasks. We keep busy so that we feel excused from getting other, more important things done.

There are many reasons why we procrastinate, such as a fear of failure or success, a lack of interest, the task is too difficult or unpleasant, and feelings of anger or hostility. However, these are not the reasons we usually give—often because we don't admit them to ourselves. We tend to give reasons like, "I don't have all the materials" or "I have to wait for information from another department" or "I have too many other commitments" or "I'm not in the mood right now, and it's not due for another week anyway" or "I work better under pressure" or "I'll get to it when I finish with this other stuff," and on and on it goes. Some of these reasons may be valid, yet underneath they are excuses.

Procrastination prevents success by keeping us busy with nonessential actions. We avoid the important but sometimes difficult or challenging tasks that are critical for obtaining the results we really want from life. Procrastination includes everything from straightening your office when you need to get that important presentation written, to watching television when you could be exercising, to avoiding a coworker rather than discussing a problem you have with him or her, to postponing activities with loved ones or children because something seems more urgent at that moment.

The first step toward getting rid of procrastination is to realize that you are in control. You make a commitment to yourself to change. Avoid defending yourself or wasting time feeling guilty. Admit what has been going on, and move in a positive direction toward your goals.

My favorite technique for overcoming procrastination is the following two-step process:

1. *Identify your procrastination rituals.* Become aware of what you tend to do when you are putting off something else. I tend to clean things I don't normally clean. And I tend to choose a time that I had scheduled for completing or starting something else. Now when I catch myself doing this, I pause and consider whether this thing really needs to be cleaned right now, or would my time be better spent on my original plan.

2. *Decide not to do the task as soon as you catch yourself procrastinating.* When you give yourself permission to *not* do the planned task, one of two things will occur within a very short time. Either you will decide to do it and wonder why you made such a big deal over it in the first place, or you will give yourself permission to not do it. In this case, the chances are that you were the only one putting pressure on yourself in the first place. Perhaps it was unrealistic to begin with.

I have found that I sometimes procrastinate when I am tired and need a break. Once I have rested, I can go back to my scheduled work with renewed energy and enthusiasm.

The following are additional techniques you might want to try. Many of these you may have heard of, but have you tried them?

■ *Take on unpleasant projects in small pieces and in short time segments.* This prevents you from feeling overwhelmed by the entire project from the outset. For example, plan to clean out one file cabinet at a time instead of your entire office. Or clean one section of the garage instead of the whole thing in one afternoon.

■ *Tell someone about it.* When we tell another person our intentions, we are more likely to complete them. The intention here is for you to keep your word to yourself, not to expect the other person to take on the responsibility of making you get the task done.

■ *Plan, schedule, and determine deadlines.* Write up a plan of what it is you want to do in detail. Then schedule time to finish either the entire project or the component parts. And give yourself deadlines for completion.

Utilizing a Master Activity List

An effective technique for keeping you on top of your activities is a master activity list. A master activity list is not your everyday to-do list, which can be self-defeating. Let's say you start the day by creating a to-do list. You have ten items on your list. Throughout the day, you cross off three items but add seven more, and tomorrow's list already has twenty items on it. How do you feel at the end of the day? Many of my clients start to feel overwhelmed.

A master activity list is an ongoing, nonprioritized list of everything you need and want to do. It is important to keep your list with you most of the time. It can be kept in your day planner, a personal digital assistant (PDA), or a small notebook in your pocket. If you have it with you all the time, you will not attempt to plan and prioritize via little bits of paper. I have a client who used to attempt to manage tasks by having reminders and notes written on torn edges of paper, sticky notes, pink message slips, napkins, and matchbook covers. He never could find what he needed or keep track of his ideas. Keep your list with you. It will allow you to jot ideas to yourself at any time, particularly when you have those great ideas but nowhere to write them.

The benefits of having a master activity list include keeping minor yet necessary tasks from slipping your mind during a hectic day; ensuring that new and innovative (as well as nice-to-do) ideas are considered all the time; facilitating comprehensive prioritization of all tasks; allowing you to consider whether new "urgent" activities are really important compared to other priorities; and, most important, listing all your activities in one place. This last benefit gives you a feeling of control over your time and reduces the feeling of being overwhelmed.

Keeping and maintaining a master activity list is the first step in the planning and scheduling process. Once you have completed a task on the list, check it or cross it off. To keep the list neat, when you have crossed off nearly all the items on a page, move the remaining items to a clean page. Some of my clients keep both personal and professional items on the same list, while others prefer to separate them. Either way, the list is a powerful technique.

Developing a Visual Plan

In Chapter 4, we examined the importance of planning and goal setting. Knowing what you want to do and what your goals are is the first important step. An additional step is necessary to reach those goals, which is to schedule your time and your tasks. Planning is determining *what* to do, while scheduling is determining *when* to do it.

A visual plan is a way to schedule your time effectively for optimum productivity. Essentially, you fill in a planner with a schedule of when you are going to work on each task that you do. Most people's calendars include only regularly scheduled meetings and appointments. The remainder of their time is left up for grabs. When you use an interoffice scheduling system, this type of calendar makes your time look wide open and encourages your coworkers to fill it in with their needs. You may have planned to get something done, but it is not on your calendar. When you fill in the spaces with the tasks you intend to perform, they can see that you are busy and will realize that you are not available.

You can use the principles of visual planning with almost any scheduling system. Many computer programs are visual in nature, but a traditional day planner, notebook, or even a flip chart will work. To plan most effectively, you need to see the week laid out in visual form. Then you can fill it in.

When you have a visual schedule, it is easier to negotiate time frames with coworkers as well as bosses. We have all had someone tell us to make time for something even after we have thoroughly explained that we truly do not have time. You need to *show* them how your time is currently scheduled, and then you can begin discussing changes. This also allows you to demonstrate the consequences.

For example, I recently had a participant share a common story. Tina was working on a project with a tight deadline and had other minor tasks that had to be completed by the end of the week. Her boss, Bob, came up to her and handed her a new project that had to be done by the end of the next day. Tina tried to explain that she did not have time, but his answer was, "Make time." Bob did not want to hear a bunch of excuses from another employee about how they did not have time to do any more work.

So, Tina dropped everything she was doing and finished the new project on time. The next day, Bob thanked her for the good work on the new project and asked about the other tasks she usually turned in on Thursdays. He wanted to know whether she would be ready for the presentation on Friday for the other big project. Tina explained that she dropped all those other things to get the new project done.

Bob couldn't believe it! The other project and reports were much more important than the one he so casually dropped in her lap. They should have been given priority. Tina explained that she just did what he ordered her to do. In this situation, neither of them came out looking good.

Does this scenario sound familiar? Both parties were miscommunicating and making assumptions. Tina assumed Bob knew what she was working on, and Bob assumed Tina knew which projects were the most important.

Ideally, you and your manager will sit down and discuss what the top priorities are in your department. Then, when you have a visual plan, you can show your boss what you are doing—no assumptions. It is not necessarily the boss's job to know what we are working on all the time. That would be micromanaging. However, it is important for us to be able to *show* what we are doing so that everyone understands the consequences of making changes. Tina needed to let Bob know what *wasn't* going to get done so that they could discuss the best plan of action.

To start your visual plan, look at a worksheet that shows a typical work week for you. See an example in Figure 5-3. Time frames are broken down into ten- to fifteen-minute intervals for each of the days of the week you typically work. This process is best done on Friday afternoons so that you can leave your work at work.

With your master activity list in hand and your goals in mind, determine what items on your list must be done in the coming week and list them on a piece of paper. If necessary, prioritize them using the paired comparison prioritizing process. Then estimate the total amount of time each item will take to complete.

The first items to put into your visual plan are your appointments and meetings and your morning and evening planning times, which are usually ten to fifteen minutes at both the beginning and end of each day. Then, put in lunch and break times. These are very important for keeping up your productivity throughout your day. Skipping or working through lunch and not taking breaks is a leading cause of burnout, accidents, illnesses, and lower productivity.

Look at your prioritized list. Write in at what time you are going to do each task. At first, you may have trouble deciding how long each task will take, but you'll soon get the hang of it.

Schedule time for responding to your mail, e-mail, and voice mail as well as for filing and general paperwork. Schedule open-door time, and let people know this is the best time for reaching you by telephone or in person. You can also use this time to make appointments with people who drop in unexpectedly and interrupt you. You pleasantly let them know that you are glad to see them, but that this is not a good time. You schedule a time to see them during your open-door time.

Figure 5-3.
Visual planning sheet.

Week of _____

	MONDAY	TUESDAY	WEDNESDAY	THURSDAY	FRIDAY
8:00AM					
8:15					
8:30					
8:45					
9:00					
9:15					
9:30					
9:45					
10:00					
10:15					
10:30					
10:45					
11:00					
11:15					
11:30					
11:45					
12:00PM					
12:15					
12:30					
12:45					
1:00					
1:15					
1:30					
1:45					
2:00					
2:15					
2:30					
2:45					
3:00					
3:15					
3:30					
3:45					
4:00					
4:15					
4:30					
4:45					
5:00					
5:15					
5:30					
5:45					
6:00					

Over time, your goal is to schedule 60 percent to 70 percent of your time, leaving 30 percent to 40 percent open and flexible, so that you can move things or add them as necessary. Keep in mind that it will take up to six months to reach this point.

For people who work in a reactive industry such as customer service, tech support, or any job that depends on outside forces, you need to switch the previous percentages. Work on planning 30 percent to 40 percent of your time, while leaving the remainder open for dealing with customers.

When considering the days of the week, you may find the following guidelines helpful. Schedule Mondays, Wednesdays, and Fridays lightly. Since you never know what is going to happen on a Monday, your plan may be useless twenty minutes after you get in if you have the day fully scheduled. Give yourself a lot of flexibility on Mondays. Wednesday is your catch-up day. A day to get back on track if Monday and Tuesday turn out to be crazier than you anticipated. You schedule Friday lightly for two reasons: (1) it can be the least productive day of the week, and (2) it is "last minute day"—the day you do all the stuff you have put off or the day your manager hands you a four-hour project at 2:30 P.M. Give yourself plenty of time on Fridays. The best-case scenario is that nothing comes up so that you have time to get ahead of things for the coming week, do some much-needed reorganizing and cleaning, and, maybe, go home early.

For most people, Tuesdays and Thursdays tend to be the most productive days of the workweek. The least number of interruptions are logged and fewer meetings are scheduled. Take advantage of these days and schedule them fairly full.

Once you have developed your plan, go home and enjoy your weekend. When you come in Monday morning, get started and stick to your plan. Spend only ten to fifteen minutes seeing what came in the mail, e-mail, and voice mail. Don't get distracted by this stuff. I know many people who start their day going through these additional in-boxes and end up losing almost an entire day. They start with the paper items, looking through the mail, responding to some memos, opening letters, flipping through catalogues while accessing e-mail, switching back and forth between the two, putting the speaker phone on and listening to voice mail messages, returning a couple e-mails, making a telephone call or two, taking care of some paper work, going to a meeting, getting caught talking to a coworker, going back to the desk to read more e-mails and listen to more voice mail messages, sending some messages and a couple reply letters, making a couple telephone calls, and on and on until the next thing you know it is 3:45 P.M. and nothing has truly been accomplished. They have been busy the entire time, but not on high-priority tasks and activities.

It is important to work your plan as much as possible. At the end of each day, review how you are doing and make any needed adjustments. Do not be surprised when you find yourself with extra time in a day. Treat yourself to a great lunch and go back to your master activity list to add to your schedule.

Creating and following a visual plan may seem simple, but most of my seminar participants and clients find it challenging at first. Remember, it will take a few months to get it to work smoothly, but you will notice progress along the way.

To Do or Not to Do? Time Logs . . .

I frequently hear people say that time logs take too much time, and they already don't have enough time to begin with. My opinion with regard to time logs is that if you know how you spend your time and can plan your day, you do not need a time log. On the other hand, if you feel that your time is out-of-control and you don't know where you spend it or if you can't even begin to create a master activity list or a visual plan of your day, take the time to make a time log. It will help. It may be the only thing that will help you to regain a sense of control.

Time logs can give you important information. For one, they help you to see all your invisible activities, which are all the things you do automatically and wouldn't notice unless they didn't get done. Second, they help you to see how long tasks actually take you to do. The best example I have seen of this is when a client of mine named Christine, who is an executive administrative professional, completed a time log. She had offered to do the copying for the office, and she found that what she thought took her no more than a couple minutes took up to half an hour. When she left her desk to make the copies, she was frequently stopped in the hall and asked questions or was asked to step into a meeting. When she got to the copier, there would often be a line or the copier was jammed or out of paper or toner. She would fix it, make her copies, and attempt to return to her desk—only to stop two to three more times on the way. Overall, she often used up thirty minutes of her day for one or two copies. After discussing the situation with her colleagues, she set up a drop-off and pickup system twice a day for all general copying. She estimates that she has regained four and a half hours in an average week.

A time log does not need to be fancy or formal. You can use a pad of paper and make a commitment to write down everything you do and the amount of time that it takes. That is all that is necessary. Time logs are for your eyes only! If you feel you have to turn them in, they won't be as accurate. Use your own system of code words, initials, and symbols.

To begin with, log a minimum of five days over a two-week period of time. Then see whether you have enough information. Most people have enough information at this point to start making changes. If you need more information, log a complete week. It will be worth it in the end. The time that you get back each week by knowing where it is wasted will more than make up for the effort.

Space

Office clutter creates the feeling of being buried. It takes you longer to locate what you need, creates distractions, and represents postponed decisions. It promotes poor prioritizing because we are tempted to pick up a task that is in view rather than a high-priority task that we might be avoiding. Clutter equals indecision. It may give us the illusion of importance as in, "Look how much I have to do—I don't have time to clean my desk," but it is a sign of poor organization.

Organizing and Streamlining Your Work Area

Imagine being able to locate the information you need—when you need it! It is easy to become frustrated when you walk into your work area and find piles of paper, mountains of messages, reams of reports, thirty-five e-mail messages waiting, stacks of reading, and your message light blinking. If your work area is cluttered and disorganized, it will lower your productivity, cause procrastination, and lead you to feeling overwhelmed and burned-out.

For some people, clutter is a way to avoid relaxing. As much as we complain about being overworked and tired, we allow clutter to mount up. In the back of our minds, we know if we remove all the clutter, we can relax. But that is scary—what will I do then? Better to always have stuff to deal with than to feel at a loss for work.

Take a good look at your work area. Decide on a plan of attack and set goals for cleaning and organizing it. You may need to start with the desktops and shelves, then move on to the files and drawers. And don't forget to clean out your computer files and floppy disks. Open every drawer and clean it out. Only put back what you use regularly. Clean the walls—maybe it is time for new artwork, pictures, or quotes.

When everything is cleaned up, determine your core work area. Is it your desktop or the area around your computer, or a combination of both? The only things you want on your work surface are a lamp, a container for writing utensils, your master list, some paper, the computer, any necessary work equipment (such as a calculator), and maybe your telephone. Use shelves for reference books and materials.

The Scan-and-Toss Process

I recommend the scan-and-toss process for dealing with all written material that comes across your desk. First, quickly scan each piece and decide whether you think you need to keep it or toss it immediately.

Next, go through and overview your keep pile. Sort these items into one of four categories: needs immediate action, need to respond, need to read, or need to file.

For items that need immediate action, take it. For items that need a response, schedule when you will reply. For items you feel you need to read, overview them first. Perhaps the overview will give you all the information you need, and you can pass it on, file it, or toss it. Thoroughly read only those documents that pertain directly to your work priorities. Date stamp the papers to be filed, and place them in your filing pending tray.

Cleaning Out Files and Drawers

Author Merrill Douglas states that, "Ninety-five percent of the things put in filing cabinets are never looked at again by anyone."[4]

I have gathered the following tips for dealing with paper and files from participants from around the world. You may also need to consider these guidelines for your computer files.

Filing Tips

File papers periodically during the week/month.

Use color-coding to separate different types of files.

Keep active files within arm's reach.

Label and archive outdated files.

Place an expiration date on all filed material.

Label everything with names that match the way you think.

If you can find things within two minutes, your system is working.

Use file-out cards if other people have access to your files.

Questions to Ask Yourself Before Filing

Is there a legal requirement for keeping this?

How will I really use this within the next year?

Do I really need it, or do I just want it?

Can I get this information again if I ever need it?

Does anyone else have a copy?

What is the worst thing that can happen if I don't keep it?

Is it useful?

Can it be put on a disk?

Would it really matter if I lost it?

Do I need all of it or only part of it?

Where will I keep it?

Moving Your In-Box

In most of the offices I visit, there are two or more trays on each person's desk for incoming mail and papers. Sometimes, there is an out-going tray as well—but I've seen them full of things that didn't appear to be on their way out!

An in-box on your desk encourages piles to form. If the box is full, people start leaving things on the middle of your desk, or on the floor, or even on your chair. With this type of setup, it is easy to misplace or lose files and papers. Remember, organization is important.

Instead of an in-box, create a vertical filing system with labels, so that you can delegate incoming information into pockets or slots. Hang pockets on the wall or door, or have a small area (not on your desk) dedicated to incoming information. At a glance, you can tell the important from the nice-to-know papers and, in some cases, know the amount of time involved for handling the work. For example, let's say a part of your job is to review expense reports. You know approximately how long it takes to review one, and you see that your pocket for expense reports is full. You will need approximately an hour and a half to complete them. Schedule the time in your calendar and rest easy, knowing you have a plan for completing them. Perhaps notify others about your scheduled time to review expense reports that week, so that stragglers get them in on time. If they don't, they will have to wait for next week's scheduled time for expense reports.

Having a vertical file organizes paper as soon as it comes through your door. Most mail can be filed by the person delivering it, thereby saving you the time it would take for you to do it. You have the benefits of clarity and organization together.

Picture a desk piled with unsorted mail and then picture a vertical file with everything automatically sorted. Picture a cluttered office and one where all the clutter is gone and everything has its place. Which feels better to you?

Even if you are the type of person who likes a bit of clutter, it is important to go through it and toss out periodically. Clutter in our physical space is draining to our mental and emotional energy. If it feels too hard to do, ask a friend or associate to help. Then perhaps you can help them. An outsider will not be sentimental about our stuff and can help us let go of things we think we "might need someday." If you haven't used it in a year, you're not going to. Keeping your work space clean and organized will go a long way in keeping you from feeling overwhelmed. Plan, set goals, and schedule when you will clear out your space. The time it takes you to do so will be returned to you ten-fold by the efficiency it brings.

Chapter 5 in Review

Stop and think about what you have read and learned in Chapter 5 that is interesting or useful to you. Fill in the diagram of the memory tree in Figure 5-4, with key words that remind you of what you learned. You may first want to write down the three main headings from Chapter 5 on the branches of the tree in Figure 5-4. Then under each branch, add your key words to fill in the details, so that you will anchor the information in your memory.

Figure 5-4.
Chapter 5 in review.

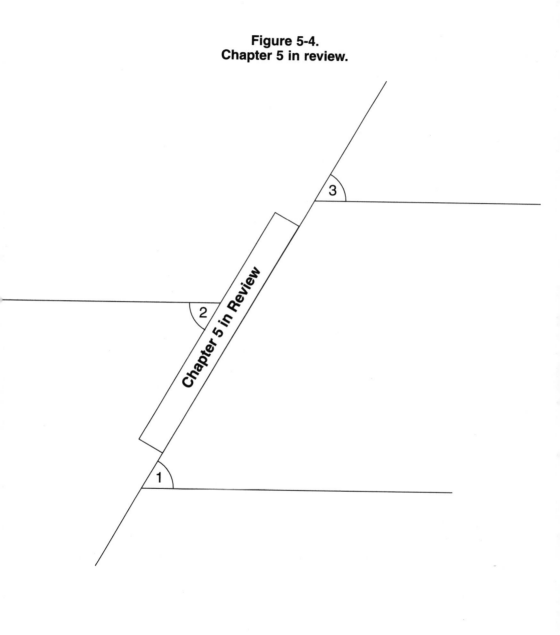

Effective Time Communication Skills

Preview Points

■ Explore internal and external communication skills.

■ Learn the A³ System for managing your self-talk.

■ Eliminate *should*'s from your vocabulary

■ Explore assertiveness skills

■ Understanding the art of saying no

Internal Communications

Internal communications, or self-talk, are the conversations that go on constantly inside our heads—what we think about the world around us, and what we think about ourselves. Most of us keep up a constant internal chatter. It is important to notice what our thoughts are and to determine whether these thoughts are generally positive or negative. And beyond this, it will substantially calm our lives and reduce our chaotic feelings if, from time to time, we can learn to quiet our thoughts.

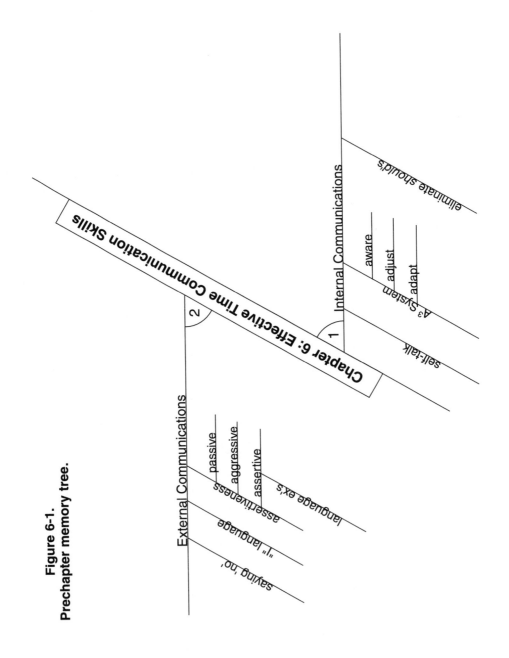

Figure 6-1.
Prechapter memory tree.

Chapter 6: Effective Time Communication Skills

1 Internal Communications
- self-talk
- A³ System
  - aware
  - adjust
  - adapt
- eliminate should's

2 External Communications
- saying 'no'
- "I" language
- assertiveness
  - passive
  - aggressive
  - assertive
- language ex's

Most of us do not realize that what we think about a situation largely determines how it affects us. We assume that how we view a matter is the way it is—not merely the way we *think* it is. However, almost any situation is open to interpretation, and the thoughts we have running through our minds—be they positive, neutral, or negative—determine our experiences in the world.

As a minor example, think about a time when you were working very hard on a project that was on deadline. You may even have had a slight headache or backache. What do you think your face looked like? More than likely you had that line between your eyebrows, your forehead was all scrunched up, and you had an intense look in your eyes.

If I walked into your office, how would I feel when you looked up at me? Depending on *my* state of mind and level of self-esteem, I would either (a) realize you were busy and come back at another time, (b) think you were angry at me, or (c) wonder what your problem was and proceed to ask my question. I would be interpreting the situation from my own emotional state.

Too often, however, we assume that our interpretation is the only one. If I thought you were angry with me, I might ask you later what I had done to offend you, and you wouldn't know what I was talking about. Meanwhile, I might have suffered a good deal worrying about the possible loss of your friendship! What a waste of time that would have been and what an unnecessary expenditure of energy. My negative interpretation of your expression caused me a night's sleep, and I never even stopped to consider that your expression had nothing to do with me. You, on the other hand, are probably wondering what my problem is.

Studies have shown that our thoughts can be negative up to 77 percent of the time. This means that the constant chatter that goes on inside your head and mine is probably not turning us into a ray of sunshine. Have you ever had thoughts like "I don't have enough time," "I never get a parking spot," "I'm always late," "I'm a slow reader," "I'm not good at math," "I can't help it, I just get angry," or "No one ever listens to me"?

We may make an assumption that these things are true because in our past someone told us this or because the people around us when we were growing up thought this way. We never stopped to examine whether these beliefs are true. Such negative thoughts run us until we notice them and decide to change them. Once we decide to make a shift, we can consciously change how we talk to ourselves and, therefore, how we see the world.

Developing Positive and Neutral Self-Talk— The A³ System

If you are constantly telling yourself that you will never get your work done or be able to catch up with it, you are right! As long as you continue to affirm these negative thoughts, they will be your reality. The A³ System helps you to shift your self-talk from negative to positive or neutral. It is a simple three-stage system: Aware, Adjust, and Adapt.

Aware

In stage one, you are becoming *aware* of what you are thinking. From time to time during your day, pause and tune in to your thoughts. What do you think about the upcoming situation, the person you are interacting with, or the person in the car in front of you? At first just notice, don't judge yourself. Become increasingly aware of your thinking. When you notice negative patterns, either write them down or notice in what situations these patterns occur.

I have a friend who was working with me in my office and I noticed that she repeatedly stated negative things about her memory. She would say things like, "My mind is like Swiss cheese," or "My mind is like a sieve," over and over again. She was mostly speaking under her breath to herself, but I noticed it. This is a perfect example of a pattern of negative thinking. She was not aware of the pattern until I brought it to her attention.

Adjust

Once you have become aware of your thinking, it is time to begin *adjusting* those thoughts. You need a method that cancels out the old thoughts from your subconscious mind. In the A³ System, you choose a word such as *erase, no, delete, cancel,* or *out* to use when you have a negative thought. You can choose whatever word works for you. It is important to repeat the word two times to yourself. Ideally, do this aloud, but if you are with others, simply say it to yourself.

In my friend's example, once I called the pattern to her attention, she started to use the word *delete* whenever she had negative thoughts about her memory. It went something like this, "My mind is like Swiss cheese," pause, "Delete. Delete." She had become aware of her thoughts and used the word delete to cancel them out.

Adapt

Stage three of the A³ System is to *adapt* a new message in place of the old negative one. You can use a positive or neutral message. Using the example of my friend, to put this all together the internal dialog would go like this:

- ■ "My mind is like a sieve." *pause*

- ■ "Delete. Delete." *pause*

- ■ "My memory is improving every day." (neutral statement) or

- ■ "My mind is in perfect order." (positive statement)

She will repeat this process every time she catches herself with the old negative thought.

These three stages work in any situation you wish to change. A system such as the A³ System is a core skill for building self-esteem. It is a simple system that you can learn to use by yourself and teach to your friends and children. Here is an example of how I have used this process when I have been feeling overwhelmed by everything I need to do:

"I'll never get all this done!" *pause*

"Cancel. Cancel." *pause*

"I'm gaining on it." (neutral) or

"I have all the time there is, and I'll get everything done that needs doing." (positive)

I have shared this system with my husband, and we *gently* remind each other of positive statements when we hear the other in a negative frame of mind. I encourage you to find others to support you in your efforts to improve your self-talk.

It is important not to expect immediate results, although you will probably start to feel better about yourself right away. Keep in mind that it takes a minimum of twenty-one to thirty days to develop a new habit or to break an old pattern. This means that it will take close to a month before you can expect the system to be solidly in place. We tend to give up on ourselves too quickly when we are changing old habits. Give yourself time. As you retrain your mind to think positively, the world will begin to look brighter from the inside out.

Eliminating *Should's*

How often do you hear yourself saying, "I *should* . . . ," or others saying to you, "You *should* . . . ?" Too often, I bet. *Should's* are demeaning to us and other people. They indicate a value judgment that makes us feel poorly about our selves when we hear it. A speaker I once heard stated it this way, "Never *should* on yourself, and whatever you do, don't *should* on other people!"

Start becoming aware of how often you say *should* to yourself and begin canceling those thoughts using the A³ System. Whenever you hear someone "shoulding" you, use the system to prevent his or her judgment from affecting you. When people say, "You should . . . ," simply repeat your canceling word two times to yourself and then respond to them in a positive way by thanking them or telling them you will keep their idea in mind. Avoid trying to explain the process to them unless they are a close friend. For example:

> **GEORGE:** Mary, you should have checked with me before you made that announcement.
>
> **MARY:** (to herself) *Cancel. Cancel.* (Out loud) Thanks for pointing that out. I'll remember next time.

Before she learned the A³ System, Mary would probably have become defensive and angry with George, thereby increasing her own distress. With the new system, she let his *should* roll off her back. If George continued to rail at her, she would merely continue the A³ System until he got tired of it. Chances are he would soon stop "shoulding" her when she didn't match his heat.

Implementing the A³ System and eliminating the *should*'s will give you control of your internal communications. Becoming conscious of your self-talk will shift how you think of yourself at home and at work. Once you let go of old self-defeating thoughts, you will be surprised at how much easier it is to focus on what you want and need to get done. Without those old negative thoughts that told you that you didn't have enough time, were not good enough, or that it *should* be different, you have more time and energy for what you *can* do.

External Communication

Once your inner voices have become friendly and supportive, it is time to work on your outer communication. It is important to work on yourself first, because you are the only person you have control over and can change. If you have been practicing positive self-talk, and have begun to communicate more effectively internally, you have probably already begun improving your external communications. Once you begin to shift the way that you respond to others, people around you will begin to shift the way they respond to you. Your inner communication directly affects your outer world. Many of your communication problems with others may already be solved.

Two of the most effective skills in communication at work are assertiveness and the ability to say no. Assertive people know where they stand and can communicate it without offending others. People who know how to say no effectively save themselves and others wasted time and energy.

Becoming More Assertive

Few of us were taught to be assertive. It is a skill most of us must learn. The styles most people use in our culture are passivity, which is when we cave in to aggressive behavior, or aggression, which is when we can act like a bully. We tend to try to get our way, not by being direct and asking for what we want—which would be a relief to everyone—but by manipulating or coercing others into giving it to us. We learned how to get what we wanted by watching other people. We used the tactics we learned from our families. Only a lucky few of us were taught by our parents how to be assertive, but it is a tactic that we can all learn. Being assertive builds self-esteem and helps us to remember that we are in control of our own needs, feelings, and desires.

It takes time to feel comfortable with assertiveness. Knowing the skills and paying attention to our emotions are the first steps toward becoming more assertive.

To get a feeling for where you fall on the scale of assertiveness look at the following continuum and place an X where you feel you would fall in most of your daily communications.

Passive- - - - - - - - - Assertive- - - - - - - - - Aggressive

To be *passive* is to allow your needs, feelings, and desires to be left unsaid or unrecognized and allows your or another's rights to be violated.

To be *assertive* means to maintain your own rights, needs, and feelings while maintaining the rights, needs, and feelings of others.

And to be *aggressive* is to violate other people's rights, needs, and feelings while maintaining your own. Please note that this type of aggressiveness is very negative, derogatory, and bullying in nature. (When business professionals are asked to be more aggressive, it usually means to be more proactive in seeking sales or reaching performance goals.)

When we are passive, we tend not to speak up for ourselves or to state what we need and want out of a given situation. Some people I meet have done this for so long that they aren't even certain what their needs are. They feel frustrated and confused because they aren't getting what they need or want out of life. Frequently, they become chronic complainers and victims of their environment.

There are degrees of passivity. The most extreme leaves us victims as described previously. Mid-level passivity is more common. Examples are not speaking up in a meeting or telling someone they are out-of-line, or feeling that we can't ask for what we want. Why don't we speak up? Many of us fear the reaction of the other person, or lack the experience to speak up confidently and calmly, or fear we will go overboard.

When we are assertive, we speak our minds in a professional, positively intentioned manner. If someone reacts strongly, we are able to understand that we did not make the other person do this, and that they are demonstrating their frustration. We understand that it does not have anything to do with us personally.

As I see it, aggressiveness falls into two categories. The first is the all-out bully. They have learned that to get their needs met, they need to shout and criticize or insult others. The second category of aggressiveness is more common. It is a more sporadic, situational aggressiveness. It usually applies when we have reached our limit. When we just can't take any more of something and lose it. We are usually more passive in our daily interactions because we do not feel comfortable or able to speak up for ourselves. Then, we get to the breaking point. After the outbreak, once we pick up the pieces, we return to our more usual behavior. Until we learn that there is another way, we seesaw between passive and aggressive behavior because it is the only way we know.

People who are very direct can also be called overly aggressive. That may be the case sometimes, but more often they are task-oriented. People who do not have the same focus can be offended, but the behavior is not meant personally. Individuals on both sides of this dilemma can help the situation by improving their skills. The overly directive person can learn to notice feelings, and the recipient of this behavior can learn not to take things personally. If you are in this kind of relationship, a communication workshop can be of great help in teaching you how to work with each other.

Language Skills to Build Assertiveness

Assertiveness can seem simple. When we see someone model assertiveness, it certainly seems easy. All we need to do is to be clear and ask for what we want. When someone asks us for something, we either say yes or no—right? Most of us have a hard time with this concept. Assertiveness training is beyond the scope of this book, but here are some tactics that assertive people use.

When you are asked a question or feel put on the spot, don't feel as though you must answer someone right away. Instead say, "Let me think about that." If it is appropriate, you can let them know when you will get back to them. What you need here is some breathing room to think before you answer—so that is what you ask for. Once you have had time to consider, you will be in a much more powerful position to reply.

When you are faced with unspecific criticism, take a breath and say, "Perhaps I could have done better. What specifically do you think needs improvement?" Our natural tendency is to defend ourselves or shut down. Instead, put the responsibility back on the person who deserves it! Unspecific criticism is extremely damaging, and you can do nothing with it. Notice you start the statement suggesting that you may have been able to do better (then again, maybe not). This tends to soothe whatever is really bothering the criticizer. And it takes the wind out of their sails. They probably expected you to defend yourself and are ready with further criticism. Once you've agreed with them, they have no place to go. This tactic is something like a martial art—instead of resisting, you use the other person's energy against them. Next, get some concrete information. If they can't provide it, know that what they said probably had nothing to do with you to begin with. You can let it go. (Easier said than done, but possible with practice.)

When you are in a situation that you believe to be unjust, try saying, "I don't feel that this is fair. Can you explain it further?" Again, you don't argue, but ask for more information. Try it instead of saying, "That's not fair!," which is likely to get you into an argument.

When someone is bullying you or throwing a temper tantrum, try saying, "Please stop. I don't allow anyone to speak to me that way." Then walk away. You may need to repeat this a couple of times. People who bully are stuck in a mental time warp of being two years old. Just keep repeating this same phrase over in a quiet and calm voice. You will get your message across.

If someone tries to buttonhole you and you are pressured for time, or are in an inappropriate place, try saying, " I don't think that this is the best time to discuss this." Then make an appointment for another time. Again, you may have to repeat yourself a few times to get through. Be pleasant and persistent. Avoid getting too upset or giving in.

Expert negotiators have a technique of assertiveness called the *broken record*. When something is very important to you and you come up against resistance, try to calmly repeat what you want, using "I" language over and over again. For example, you might say, "I understand that is the common policy. I still request a review of the issue." Often, they will come back at you with the standard policy over and over again. You stay calm, and you repeat, "I understand that is the common policy. I still request a review of the issue." Do not back down until you get your review or a satisfactory answer. You will be surprised at how well this technique works.

Using "I" Language

Most of us have at least heard about using "I" language when we want to communicate our feelings to another person. On the surface it seems so logical, but it is not usually in our training. Instead of saying what we need or want, we focus on what the other person is doing to us. Instead of taking ownership of our feelings or wants, we try to make the other person wrong.

For example, in many offices, people use their speakerphones as a regular habit rather than picking up the receiver. In today's shared workspace environment, this can be very distracting. The assertive way to approach this situation is to pick a time when things are calm and talk to the person. You can say something like this, "When you use the speakerphone, I can hear you and it distracts me from my work. I'd appreciate it if you'd use the handset." What usually happens is that we wait until we are fed up and we use "you" language instead. It usually goes like this, "Can't you see people are trying to work here! Turn the blankety-blank thing off, why don't you!"—or something to this effect. We've set up a situation where we have antagonized a person with whom we have to work closely.

When I recommend "I" language in my seminars, participants often think it is rude. They can't imagine making such a request. What we need to understand is that using "I" language prevents and solves problems, whereas "you" language creates blame, shame, and retaliation. "I" language is the cornerstone of being assertive.

Wherever you find yourself on the scale from passive to aggressive, these techniques can help. It will take some time before you are comfortable using them, or even remember to use them. At first, there may be a time lag between an occurrence and your ability to come up with an assertive reaction. This is natural. The first step to becoming assertive is to recognize when you can use your new skills. Your old way of reacting will dominate. However, once the situation is over, recreate it in your mind—the way you wish it had gone. Go over it repeatedly, seeing yourself reacting assertively. Eventually, the new picture will overtake the old one. You will notice that the gap between a situation and an assertive response will narrow. Over time, the gap gets smaller until you recognize a situation immediately and are naturally assertive. You know how to respond in the moment. The first time you use assertiveness techniques you will probably still feel shaky inside, but do it anyway. You'll feel great afterward!

Confidently Saying No

How easy is it for you to say no? Can you say it without feeling guilty or expecting an angry response? Why is it so hard for most of us to say? Most likely because we have not been taught how to do it well. To most of us, the word *no* is a four-letter word. Yet, saying no in an assertive manner can be a positive experience for all involved. Saying no with clarity and kindness can protect you from doing something that is not your job and can save you time to do the work that is yours.

Many of us can only say no to a request when we are desperate or angry—when we have reached our limit of endurance—and then it becomes a negative experience. Often, our only experience of someone saying no has been hurtful or negative. We see the person as having an attitude problem, and we certainly don't want to be like that!

I am always amazed when an adult says to me that they can't possibly say no to their boss because they would get fired or get into big trouble. It is as if the boss were an all-powerful being with complete control over their lives.

In the ever-increasing chaos of our working environments, it is imperative to learn to say no. You need to recognize the consequences of continuing to agree to do more than you can handle (I'm sure you are already aware of them if you are reading this book) and realize that you must set limits. Success is all in the delivery of your message.

Here is a three-step process to help you say no. The first step is to acknowledge the request. If appropriate, thank the person for asking you and then say you will check your schedule and get back to them in a specified amount of time. If they want an immediate answer, reassure them that you will get back to them. Tell them that you must consult your schedule to see whether there are any conflicts and to check your availability. Some people may still complain, particularly those who have always gotten an immediate yes from you in the past. Know that it will take time to retrain them. They will soon learn that you are not always immediately available to them.

Step two is to determine what you want to do. You may want to say yes. So, you ask, why didn't I just say yes in the first place? Because you are breaking people and yourself of the habit of giving answers without thinking first. If you need to say no, you will have the time to think out the reasons for your answer. Check your schedule, consult your priorities, and keep your goals in mind. If you need to reschedule other tasks or to change deadlines, make a note of them.

Step three is saying yes or no. Again, if appropriate, you may want to thank the person for asking. If it is a request that you need to say no to, say that your schedule is full or that you have a previous commitment. These are not excuses that will be challenged. If they are so bold as to ask what you are doing, you may want to ask them why they need to know.

If the request is from a boss or coworker and a direct no is not possible, it is time to negotiate. Here is where you will need your schedule notes from step two. Explain that you will be happy to do the task but need to discuss the timing with them. Perhaps even show them your schedule (don't be surprised when they are amazed at everything you do) and let them know the consequences of your shifting your schedule of tasks.

A frequent problem I see is that people assume that their bosses know all that they are doing. Bosses, on the other hand, assume that we would not agree to do something if it would jeopardize another important task or a deadline on another project. Discuss how your schedule will shift in order to accommodate their request. Keep your tone professional. Threatening or whining never helps. Even if you both decide that you can acquiesce to their request, you have set a precedent. With your negotiation you have set new limits and boundaries. Each time you do so, it will get easier.

Another way to say no gracefully is to suggest an alternative—an alternative time, person, department, or even suggest that they might do it themselves. You may have been the one to fix the copier in the past, but you no longer have time. You can suggest that maintenance do it or that *they* contact the service provider. This option is best when we have gotten into the habit of doing work that is not in our job description. In the past we may have had time to do these things, but we no longer do. We may be the one who knows the answers or knows where things are kept, but the interruptions are interfering with our productivity. Break others of the habit of coming to you for this information. This does not mean you cannot be helpful sometimes, but these types of interruptions eat away your time during the day.

A large part of our feelings of chaos comes from feeling that we have no control over our time. Learning to be assertive and learning how to say no will not only save you time but will prevent you from feeling like a victim of other people's priorities.

Once you have discovered what you value, have set goals, become more organized, and have taken control of your internal and external communications, you will feel as though your work life is in your own hands—and competent hands at that!

Chapter 6 in Review

Stop and think about what you have read and learned in Chapter 6 that is interesting or useful to you. Fill in the diagram of the memory tree in Figure 6-2 with key words that remind you of what you learned. You may first want to write down the two main headings from Chapter 6 on the branches of the tree in Figure 6-2. Then under each branch, add your key words to fill in the details so that you will anchor the information in your memory.

Figure 6-2.
Chapter 6 in review.

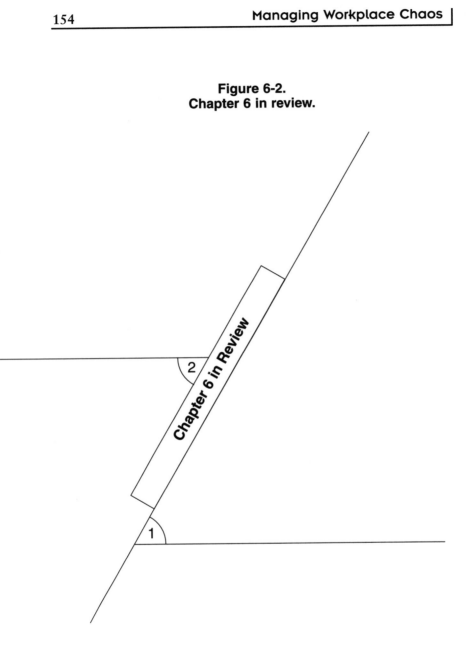

PART THREE
Keeping Life Balanced

The information you have read in Part 1 and Part 2 on how to manage information and time efficiently can help you to avoid the work overload and stress that cause burnout. However, patterns of overwork can be hard to break, especially when we have a strong work ethic or are the type A personality that must be busy all the time.

Some readers may feel burned-out already. If that is true, nearly everything seems like too much effort to you right now. This is not the time to force yourself to try new things or to restructure your work life. You do not have the emotional or mental capacity to make changes. First, you need to arrange some time for yourself. No matter how impossible it may seem, take some time off from work. If your family life is chaotic, ask for help and go off by yourself—if only for a weekend. It is nearly impossible to make changes or to learn new skills when you are already beyond your limit.

The Burnout Factor

Preview Points

- Identify your current level of burnout.
- Learn the four stages of burnout.
- Explore self-care solutions for each stage.

How often do you comment on how overworked and tired you are? Are you bragging or complaining? In our culture, many of us gauge our value on how much work we do. I see people in organizations almost bragging about how burned-out they are, as if it were some type of contest that you won by collapsing from exhaustion. Some businesses value and promote workers who put in hours of overtime and act as though they are married to the company. Is this what we really want for ourselves? What message is this sending to the next generation?

Burnout can occur at any time in our lives. Today, more than ever before, U.S. workers are experiencing burnout—and organizations and families are left trying to cope with the ashes. At some point, when many of us are young, we get the idea that work is supposed to be all-encompassing and stressful. It could be the

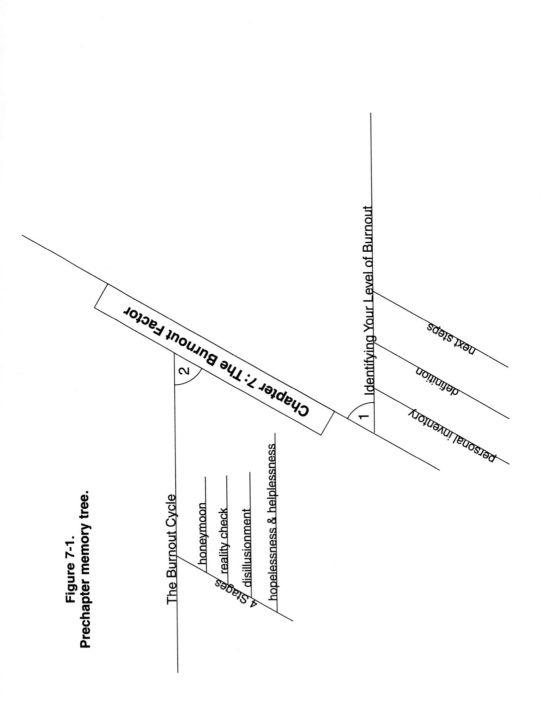

Figure 7-1.
Prechapter memory tree.

Chapter 7: The Burnout Factor

1 Identifying Your Level of Burnout
- personal inventory
- definition
- next steps

2 The Burnout Cycle
- 4 Stages
  - honeymoon
  - reality check
  - disillusionment
  - hopelessness & helplessness

message and example we get from our parents, our experience of school carried over to work, or the Puritan work ethic that is prevalent in our culture, which stresses the virtue of work over play.

I recently taught a management class at an e-commerce organization where most of the management were recent (within three to five years) graduates of Harvard and Yale business schools. The average age of the participants was 29. When we were discussing motivating factors and mentoring techniques for their direct reports, there was a great deal of complaining about how lazy the employees were and how they had a lack of commitment to the company. When I asked them to give me examples, almost all of the managers stated how the employees went home by 6:00 P.M. and rarely came in before 8:00 A.M. I asked what the standard working hours were and I was told 9:00 A.M. to 5:00 P.M. These people were working overtime—but not enough for these overachievers!

The managers were unhappy that most of their staff wanted to work standard hours. When I pointed this out and asked if it was true, they paused for a second and said yes. After all, they worked an average of seventy to eighty hours a week because that is the way it is supposed to be. I asked them who said it was supposed to be that way. I received no answer.

These young managers felt duty-bound to work a great deal of overtime and to feel stressed out. The more I worked with them, the more I saw that if they did not feel rushed and pressured, they did not feel productive. Unfortunately, because of their intensity, they had a very high turnover of employees and wasted a lot of time because of miscommunications and ineffective work. I wonder what they will be like ten years from now.

These young men and women are not unusual. Many of us get into a similar pattern and stay in it. Most of us believe that our success depends on overwork. Yet no matter how successful we become, our minds and our bodies can handle this intense stress only for a limited amount of time until burnout occurs.

Burnout causes lower productivity, loss of accountability, job absenteeism, on-the-job injuries, and escalating illnesses in workers. Not to mention the stress it causes in the home. In the past, most businesses considered overwork to be the mark of a successful employee and burnout an inevitable by-product, but ideas are beginning to turn around. Studies are showing that workers who live a more balanced life are more productive, less inclined toward illness, and better all-around employees.

Still, until we begin to live in the best of all worlds, we will be dealing with the causes of burnout. In Part 3, you will have the opportunity to gauge your level of burnout, understand the stages, and take a look at the stress levels in your life right now. We will then cover some ideas on what you might do to begin balancing your life to be in alignment with your goals.

Identifying Your Level of Burnout

The effects of stress are cumulative. We all live within stress levels that keep us active and energized. However, when we tip the scales too often, we can lose our balance and our ability to keep up and bounce back. When this happens we start to experience burnout.

To get a feel for the indicators of burnout and to see how you are doing, complete the following exercise. Please review each of the issues and circle the number that reflects your feelings over the last three months. Number 1 is low (I have not experienced this) and 4 is high (I feel this way a lot of the time lately).

1 2 3 4   Complaining of fatigue, overwork, being exhausted

1 2 3 4   Loss of enthusiasm, energy, drive, and team spirit

1 2 3 4   Fighting changes, being inflexible, rigid, and unyielding

1 2 3 4   Becoming defensive easily, allowing key relationships to deteriorate

1 2 3 4   Getting disorganized, accident-prone, having poor recall and memory

1 2 3 4   Rationalizing, passing the buck, and withdrawing

1 2 3 4   Feeling less of a sense of satisfaction about your performance

1 2 3 4   Working harder and harder but accomplishing less

1 2 3 4   Feeling more cynical and disenchanted with your work and the people you work with

1 2 3 4   Getting more irritable, angry, and short-tempered with the people around you

1 2 3 4   Having more physical complaints than normal

1 2 3 4   Feeling that you just don't have anything more to give to yourself or anyone else

To determine your score, add up the total of the numbers you circled. For example, first count up all the times you circled the number 1 in that column and add them together, then the count all the times you circled the number 2 and add them together, then do the same for the numbers 3 and 4. Now add all your column totals together for a grand total.

Now take a look at what your results may represent. Remember it isn't the total number that counts as much as the insight you gain by responding to the statements.

If you scored 12 to 22: You are in good shape! You may want to start paying attention; however, you don't have much to worry about. We can all have these problems from time to time—just as long as you're not having too many of them at the same time.

If you scored 23 to 35: You may be in early- to mid-level stages of burnout. You have the opportunity to bounce back before you get too hot and start to burn out—but don't put it off! Things tend to get worse from here if you don't start taking action to bring some balance back into your life now.

If you scored 36 to 48: You are on the edge of mid-level to full burnout and are likely to experience an involuntary major life change. Start making time for yourself today.

The Four *D*'s of Danger

A quick indicator of impending burnout are the four *D*'s of danger: *D*isorganization, *D*ecision making, *D*epression, and *D*ependency.

Disorganization is self-explanatory. Can you find anything in your office within two minutes? Do you know what your schedule looks like for next week? Or have you begun to forget appointments and started misplacing things? Do you *feel* disorganized?

How about decisions? Are you able to make them? Or do you feel that it is too difficult to make up your mind lately?

What about depression? Are you glad to face each new day? Or is it harder to get up in the morning?

And dependency. Are you somewhat independent, or are you needing people or comfort foods more than normal? Are you usually resilient, or do you become emotional over the slightest thing?

As you read in the article from Chapter 1, experiencing these symptoms or a combination of them that is *more than normal* for you, is an early warning signal that you need to slow down a bit and do some self-care. Take breaks during the day, get some time for yourself on the weekends, and get back on track.

More Indicators of Stress and Burnout

Take a moment and analyze yourself. Do you move rapidly all the time? Are you impatient with the speed at which most events take place? Do you want to hurry up others? Try to do more than two things at once? These behaviors are sometimes attributed to type A personalities, but I think we can all fall victim to this "busyness" in today's fast-paced world. Start making a conscious effort to slow down. Remember to take stock periodically. Stop and smell the roses!

What Burnout Represents

There is all this talk about burnout, but what is it? *Burnout,* as defined by Ayala Pines and Elliot Aronson in their book *Career Burnout: Causes and Cures,* is

> a state of physical, emotional, and mental exhaustion caused by long-term involvement in situations that are emotionally demanding. People who suffer burnout exhibit an array of symptoms—physical depletion and feelings of helplessness, hopelessness, and disillusion. They develop a negative concept of themselves and negative attitudes toward their work, those involved in the work, and even life itself.[1]

My mother and father were examples of early burnout. My father was only in his late twenties when he had been working for a large computer manufacturer in New England for six years. He had received promotion upon promotion with the accompanying increasing responsibilities. He had recently bought a house and was the sole financial support for our family. He had been working on a project for eighteen months when it was suddenly canceled. All his work went down the drain.

My mother, on the other hand, was deeply into volunteerism. She was scheduled to chair a committee the next year that she did not even want to be on. Neither of them felt that they could do anything about their situations other than to completely start over again. Their solution was to drop everything and move to Florida to run a garden center with my father's family. It took my father four years of potting plants and bagging dirt in the hot sun before he was ready to return to the computer industry.

What Can You Do?

Determine to find a sense of importance in something besides work. Develop your sense of satisfaction in life. Understand your priorities and set goals for achieving a life that represents those priorities. Place your work into the overall perspective of your life and keep it there. Remember the value of the other factors in your life, including your spouse or partner, children, hobbies, friends, and your health.

The Burnout Cycle

The burnout cycle can occur at any time. When we start a new project, get a new job, welcome a new baby home, or when we have taken on too much at work or at home—whenever we go beyond the limits of our ability to cope successfully—we tend to enter the burnout cycle.

The following are the four stages of the burnout cycle:

1. The honeymoon

2. The reality check

3. Disillusionment

4. Hopelessness and helplessness

Just because you are in the cycle does not mean you are doomed to end up at stage four. At any time, you can begin to do self-care and pull yourself out. Few of us stay in the honeymoon stage, so it is not realistic to expect to stay there. However, if we take the steps necessary for self-care, we can level off at stage two, which is the reality check, and remain there.

STAGE ONE   The Honeymoon

In stage one, we are wearing rose-colored glasses and everything seems perfect—the perfect job, perfect person, or perfect project. We enjoy the idiosyncrasies of our coworkers, we laugh at the silly things the new person in our life does, we are excited about the new project and envision a wonderful end result. The key to stage one is to enjoy it, *for now*. Remember that it is temporary. Put all that excess energy to work for you. But, we need to remember that life was not intended to be like the movies—it would be exhausting!

To maintain balance in stage one, it is a good idea to find out what happened before you came into the picture. Why did the last person leave the job you were recently hired for? (Were they taken out on a stretcher? Were they promoted? Go to another company?)

Let's look at the new person in your life. (What happened in his or her last relationship? Was it an awful breakup or a mutual decision?)

If this is your first big project, find out what happens during big projects at this company. (Do they make major changes halfway through? Or lack project-planning skills so that there is always a deadline rush?)

Not that any of these things will happen to you, but the information will be helpful in preparing you for all eventualities. It can prevent you from becoming disillusioned farther down the road.

STAGE TWO The Reality Check

This is when we come to realize that not everything is perfect. We begin to realize what we are up against. Some of those idiosyncrasies of our coworkers, the silly things the new person in our life does, and the some of the aspects of the new project are becoming annoying and tedious.

To maintain balance in stage two, it is important to resolve issues as they arise and work on accepting some things as they are. We need to discuss the small things that others do that irritate us *now*. Keep in mind, you are not attempting to change the other person but to make your needs and feelings known. If a coworker makes inappropriate jokes or is always speaking loudly on the speakerphone, you need to talk with the person about it ASAP. We tend to put these types of discussions off because we don't want to make a big deal out of a relatively small issue, and we are probably uncomfortable bringing it up. But these are the types of things that we explode over when under pressure. The time to discuss it is now. You can practice some of the assertiveness skills you learned in Part 2, such as using "I" statements and asking for what you want.

Also, try to accept some things as they are. Think of a time you bought something at a store that was marked "as is." What did that mean? Exactly—you accepted the item with its open box, scratches, stains, dents, or tears. It is the same with people and organizations. You may not like the way a person does something or agree with the policies of an organization. You may prefer another way. You can make your feelings known, but that is it. They don't have to change because you don't like it. This is where acceptance comes in. To accept does not mean to agree or approve. It simply means you are not going to give any more energy to struggling against what is. Save your energy for the big issues. You accept the situation with its inherent problems.

Stage two is the leveling-off stage where most of life's events occur. If you handle problems as they arise, use "I" language, and learn to accept what you cannot change while you are in stage two, you prevent stress from accelerating toward burnout.

STAGE THREE Disillusionment

If we haven't taken the steps necessary for maintaining balance in stage two, we are at risk of entering stage three. This stage begins with self-doubt and blame. We may have ignored the small problems that arose in stage two or we may have too many things happening at once in our lives. Perhaps we have gotten a wake-up call from a loved one demanding a change or we suddenly have a serious health issue. There are two options in stage three: We either become proactive and move back to stage two or we become reactive and move on to stage four.

What you can do during the initial phase of stage three is to realize that it is not as bad as it seems. If you catch yourself early enough, you can utilize your internal resources and regain a sense of balance. This is what I call option one.

In option one of stage three, you reevaluate your situation and take responsibility for your part of what is happening (we always have a part to play in this). You learn how to speak assertively with others about the situation. If you are able to do this, you can reprioritize yourself and your work and get back on track.

Sometimes, stage three is a surprise to us because we have been running full steam ahead and not paying attention to the warning signs along the way. When this is the case, we can end up in option two.

If we have not been proactive, stress keeps building and we start to see everything as a problem. We become externally focused, blaming others and outside circumstances for everything that seems to be going wrong in our lives. We are unable to see solutions. We can sometimes feel a great sense of betrayal and distress that others do not see things our way. Option two leads to stage four.

STAGE FOUR Hopelessness and Helplessness

We feel like giving up. We simply can't do it all anymore. Or we may feel angry and take that anger out inappropriately on others. Serious health problems tend to occur at this stage.

What can you do if you find yourself in stage four? It is time to reevaluate and reprioritize your life. Take a time-out, go away for a long weekend to get started or take a couple of weeks to gear down and decide on the changes you need to make. You may even wish to seek professional support. But remember that you need skills, not just pills—medication is only a temporary, although sometimes necessary, fix. Chances are, if you don't take a time-out, your body will arrange one for you. You'll end up with a serious injury or severe illness that puts you in bed for an extended period of time. No one wants it to go this far, but in the chaos of today's workplace, this is an increasingly common occurrence.

Recovery is possible at all stages in the cycle. One key is to give yourself permission to take care of yourself. I know many people who only feel justified calling in sick to work when they literally cannot get out of bed. Avoid this by making you and your well-being a priority. Trust me, your organization will not come to a screeching halt if you are not there. If you left today, they would be able to replace you. I do not say this to diminish your value, but to remind you that it is okay to take time for yourself. If you don't take care of yourself, who will? Remind yourself that you are doing everyone a favor by staying well-balanced and healthy. A side benefit is that you will become a model for others in your life, demonstrating for them a new and positive paradigm for living.

Chapter 7 in Review

Stop and think about what you have read and learned in Chapter 7 that is interesting or useful to you. Fill in the diagram of the memory tree in Figure 7-2 with key words that remind you of what you learned. You may first want to write down the two main headings from Chapter 7 on the branches of the tree in Figure 7-2. Then under each branch, add your key words to fill in the details so that you will anchor the information in your memory.

Figure 7-2.
Chapter 7 in review.

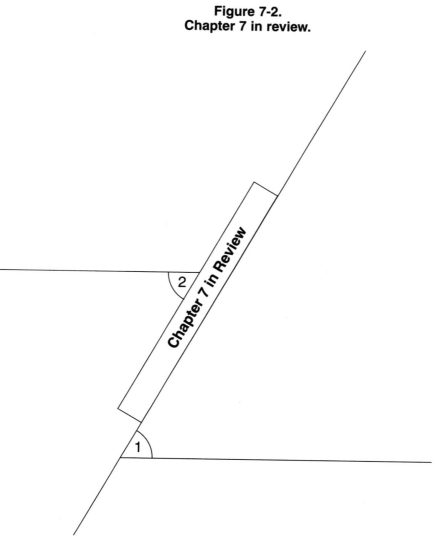

CHAPTER 8

Take a Look Back at Your Stressors . . . And Ahead at Balance

Preview Points

- Complete three stress inventories.

- Review and understand your scores.

- Learn coping strategies for the different types of stressors in your life.

The body is a finely tuned instrument that responds to its environment. This includes all the physical, mental, and emotional factors in your life. Any sudden change in your surroundings or change in your routines can cause stress.

As a general rule, stress is not inherently negative. As Dr. Hans Selye, pioneering biological scientist, describes it in *Stress Without Distress*, "Stress is the nonspecific response of the body to any demand made upon it."[1] In other words, being alive is a stress. Selye says that "the complete absence of stress equals death."[2] I remind my participants in stress management courses that death is not our goal.

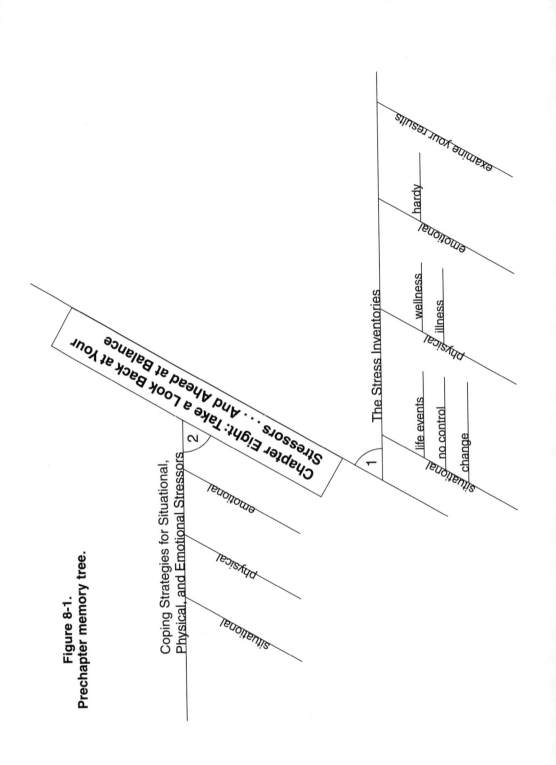

Figure 8-1.
Prechapter memory tree.

Chapter Eight: Take a Look Back at Your
Stressors . . . And Ahead at Balance

The Stress Inventories

1

situational
life events
no control
change

physical
wellness
illness

emotional
hardy

examine your results

2

Coping Strategies for Situational,
Physical, and Emotional Stressors

situational

physical

emotional

We all know that what is difficult for one person is simple for another. It is the same with positive and negative stress. Our perceptions cause us to feel positive or negative about any given situation. When stress is a positive factor in our lives, we tend to feel energized, focused, and motivated. When stress is a negative factor, we tend to feel angry, tense, and frustrated.

A stressor is the person or event that we perceive as causing us stress—be it positive or negative.

First, you will informally score yourself on three stress indicators. Then, we will examine the results and explore options for helping you with problem areas.

The Stress Inventories

The following three stress inventories will guide you in determining the types of stress that are currently influencing your life. Ideally, the inventories will give you insight as to where you need to focus to keep your life in balance. Many people are surprised at their results. Some, who think they have many stressors in their lives find they have only a few—but they are major and therefore the effects are intense. Others are surprised at how many stressors they are dealing with, but they are not as affected by them because the stressors are minor.

The intention of these inventories is not to give you a medical diagnosis. I offer them only as a guide for gaining insight into the stressors in your life. Once you have completed and scored all the inventories, we will review the results.

Situational Stress Inventory

The situational stress inventory focuses on major life events. Life events may be interpreted as positive or negative stressors. What is important to recognize in this inventory is that every major life event causes a change in your normal routine. It is this change that acts as a stressor. In the life event inventory, we will uncover the events in your life that cause stress. In the physical and emotional stress inventories, we will discover how well you are able to handle these events.

To complete the life event inventory, review the following twenty life events. If the event occurred in the past six months or you expect it to occur in the next three months, place a check mark next to the impact score for that event. Remember, it doesn't matter if you view these events as good or bad, only note that they have occurred or that you expect that they will occur.

LIFE EVENT	IMPACT SCORE
Death in the family	.90
Divorce	.90
Marital separation	.80
Personal injury or illness	.80
Marriage	.80
Loss of work	.80
Pregnancy in household	.70
Change in responsibility at work	.60
Outstanding personal achievement	.40
Injury or illness in a close family member	.60
Trouble with boss or coworkers	.50
Moving	.60
Spouse begins or stops working	.50
Change in sleeping habits	.30
Vacation	.40
Change in eating habits	.30
Holidays	.60
Commuting difficulties	.60
High debt	.50
Crime victimization	.80

Add up the impact scores of all the events you checked and place the total score here _____ .

Physical Stress Inventory

The physical stress inventory measures how susceptible you are to physical stress. Essentially, this inventory indicates how well you take care of yourself on a regular basis.

To complete this inventory, score each item on a scale from 1 to 10. A score of 1 means, "Yes, this is true for me regularly," while a score of 10 means, "No, this is not true for me."

1. I look forward to starting each new day.
2. I have a network of friends and acquaintances.
3. I eat at least one balanced meal a day.
4. I have adequate income to meet my expenses.
5. I am in good health (including eyesight, hearing, and teeth).
6. I do not use medications or chemicals to help me sleep.
7. I exercise to the point of perspiration at least twice a week.
8. I get strength from my spiritual beliefs.
9. I have a place where I can relax and be by myself.
10. I actively pursue a hobby.
11. I do something fun at least once a week.
12. I do not smoke and I do not drink more than three alcoholic drinks a week.
13. I am happy in my current job/career/work.
14. I get along well with my coworkers.
15. I eat healthy foods (low in fat, sugar, and salt).
16. I have a supportive family.
17. I sleep well and wake up refreshed.
18. I belong to a social group that meets regularly.
19. I can openly speak about my feelings when angry or worried.

20. I am less than twenty pounds over or under a healthy weight for my body style.

Total up your scores and place the total here: _____

Emotional Stress Inventory

The emotional stress inventory measures your hardiness level. In other words, your ability to bounce back from life's pressures and problems.

Place a check mark in the box next to each statement to indicate whether you mostly agree or disagree.

AGREE   DISAGREE

❏   ❏   1. I enjoy new situations and seek them out.

❏   ❏   2. I make sure I have at least one day a week when I have nothing planned.

❏   ❏   3. What I do is important and makes a difference in my world.

❏   ❏   4. I talk about my feelings with the people I am close to.

❏   ❏   5. When things change suddenly in my life, I welcome the challenge.

❏   ❏   6. What I do is more important than how much I am paid.

❏   ❏   7. I would give up my job to do something more interesting to me.

❏   ❏   8. I am an autonomous person, I make the decisions about what affects me.

❏   ❏   9. An average person can make a difference.

❏   ❏   10. I have the power and ability to be a success in my field.

❏   ❏   11. I like to get up each day to see what the world has to offer me.

❏   ❏ 12. I know I am in charge of how I react in a
             situation.

❏   ❏ 13. What others do doesn't "get" to me.

❏   ❏ 14. I am confident when speaking to other
             people.

❏   ❏ 15. I don't allow aggressive people to upset me.

Count up the number of check marks you placed in the
agree column and place that total here _____.

Examine Your Results

You have now informally scored yourself on three major
scales that will give you a picture of where you may be
experiencing a lack of balance. Now we can examine
what your numbers mean. Keep in mind that the numbers
are not as important as the indication of areas of stress in
your life.

First, take a moment to record your results from the previous section in the place provided for each inventory.

Situational Stress Total _____

0–300	Average levels of change
301–600	Moderate levels of change
601–900	High levels of change
901–1,200	Extreme levels of change

The levels of change indicated on this inventory give you
insight as to how many life events are occurring for you
now. The higher the number, the more care you need to
take. Avoid overloading yourself with other activities. Many
of these events are beyond your control. If you are emotionally susceptible and your hardiness is low (see other
inventories), even one or two of these events can throw you
off balance. The numbers are not good or bad; they are
merely showing you how much change you are dealing

with. We have become accustomed to dealing with so much in our lives that we may not be aware of all that we are currently handling. Use this information as a guide to give yourself permission to take care of your priorities.

Physical Stress Total _____

20–65	Slightly Susceptible
66–110	Somewhat Susceptible
111–155	Seriously Susceptible
156–200	Extremely Susceptible

In this inventory, the term susceptible refers to having physical symptoms of stress such as headaches, stomachaches, backaches, irritability, impatience, and intolerance. Do not assume that these symptoms are normal. They tend to escalate and become more severe the longer we ignore them.

Emotional Stress Total _____

0–5	Low Hardiness
6–10	Moderate Hardiness
11–15	Hardy

In this inventory, hardiness refers to the ability to keep up with life's pressures. The lower your hardiness score, the fewer resources you have to cope with change. You tend to have less ability to fight off illness and mental anxiety.

Coping Strategies for Situational, Physical, and Emotional Stressors

You now have an understanding of what types of stressors are currently affecting you. Remember, this is a current picture. Retake the inventories in three to six months and notice how they change.

Knowing what types of stress you are dealing with is the first step toward reclaiming balance in your life. For many of my participants, just getting a clear picture of these issues goes a long way in reducing their stress. Once they can "see" what is going on, it doesn't feel quite so overwhelming. Many are able to then give themselves permission to ease up on themselves.

Situational Coping Strategies

Situational stressors are events and situations over which we have little to no control. Whether it is one or several of these events, it can throw us for a loop, especially when our lives are already chaotic. Remember, we may label these events as positive or negative. That label does not change the amount of upheaval the event can cause in our life.

Here are four suggestions to help you stay balanced during times of intense situational stress. The first is organization. Use the techniques you learned in Part 2 to help you get and stay organized. It is important when we are dealing with situational stress to have a personal organizational plan to keep track of our days. Always have your notebook, date book, or personal digital assistant (PDA) at hand.

The second suggestion is to have a purposeful vision for your life. Sometimes it is hard to understand why things happen the way they do. We can become discouraged and start to feel hopeless when tragedy strikes, such as when a loved one is hurt or lost to us. We can also feel overwhelmed when we begin to realize the amount of work that is involved in planning a vacation, starting a new business, or the arrival of a new baby. Having a purposeful vision for your life will help you to remember your personal guiding principles when you feel like striking out at the world. For example, a vision I have for myself is to have all my interactions with other people result in positive or neutral outcomes. This helps me to remember to be aware of my behavior in difficult times, so I do not say or do something I will later regret.

When I am traveling and encounter flight cancellations and delays, I can find myself feeling tired, frustrated, and cranky. If it is the end of a long training week, all I want to do is go home. My temptation is to react out of my feelings. I want to lash out at the airport staff for something they have no control over. My internalized value reminds me to pause, breathe, and reset my attitude.

When we have a special event coming up in our lives, or a special project we are working on, it is important to keep our focus on the vision of what we want to accomplish. In the midst of all the work that is involved, our vision will help us through the rough spots.

For example, visioning a beautiful healthy baby will get you through the morning sickness, awkwardness, and any sacrifices you need to make. Imagining your satisfied customers will help you with the challenges of starting up a business.

The third suggestion is to utilize or generate supportive relationships. Be in contact with people who are purely supportive of your current situation. They aren't telling you what you should do or how to do things. Supportive people ask questions to understand your needs and wants and they have your best interests in mind. Supportive people also understand when you need to be alone. They don't hold resentments when you need to say no. Give yourself the gift of receiving from others when you need it.

Sometimes you can find support in strangers by joining a group. Whether in person or online, you can find a group that focuses on the situation you are dealing with. Check community bulletin boards at libraries and hospitals and check in your telephone book, or go online and conduct a search.

The fourth suggestion is to develop and maintain daily rituals. Daily rituals give us a sense of stability when we have changes occurring in our lives. You already have many daily rituals, such as your morning and nighttime routines. Some additional daily rituals that you may find helpful are walking, yoga, meditation, prayer, inspirational reading, being outdoors, spending time with pets, or spending a few minutes in a place that is soothing to you. It does not matter what you choose as your ritual, as long as it has a calming effect on you.

It is important that you do this ritual every day at the same time, no matter where you are. Whether I am at home or traveling, I start every day with a silent time of meditation and inspirational reading with a lit candle. This ritual starts my day off in a positive and unhurried manner. If I happen to miss a day for some reason, I notice that the day does not go as smoothly or that I have a harder time handling daily frustrations.

If you don't already have a daily ritual, start trying out some of the previous suggestions. Your ritual doesn't have to take very long—maybe only a minute at the end of your shower in the morning to clear your thoughts and to be grateful for what you have.

Physical Coping Strategies

When the inventory suggests you may be susceptible to suffering from the physical symptoms of stress, such as headaches, stomachaches, backaches, irritability, impatience, and intolerance, here are three suggestions to help you regain balance.

First, make certain that you are eating well and exercising. I'm sure you have heard this many times, but do you do it? I'm not suggesting you go on a special diet or begin a stressful exercise routine. You can begin by merely paying attention to what you eat and taking a brief walk during the day. You may be surprised how quickly you begin to feel better with only a few minor changes. Small changes can lead to bigger ones. You may soon feel a desire to develop a program that brings you to optimal health.

The second suggestion is to get some rest and allow self-care into your life. When physical stress hits, it can be difficult to get motivated to do anything. We easily become cranky and moody. Do you get enough sleep? Do you take time for yourself? How about a hobby or volunteer activity? Remember that physical stress tends to escalate if we don't take action to offset it. To prevent serious consequences, you must make yourself and your health a priority.

The third suggestion for coping with physical stress is to have goals that you are successfully working toward. Refer to the goal section in Chapter 4 as a guide for writing effective goal statements. Having goals helps you to remember what your priorities are when you are under stress. They keep you moving forward on your life's plan. You will feel less burdened by the external chaos of life when you have goals to guide you.

I encountered an extreme case of physical stress in one of my training programs. Three quarters through the first day, I had a participant put her head down on the desk and say that the program was too much for her. I had noticed that she had come to the office two hours ahead of the scheduled start of the program, and I overheard her saying that she hadn't had time for breakfast. She had only a Danish and coffee during the break. She worked through lunch and ate only a bag of corn chips and a soda. I found out that she had recently returned early from maternity leave, was working sixty-five hours a week, and was attempting to breast-feed her baby. Just before her afternoon meltdown, she had a cookie during the break.

It was only after I had shared my observations about her behavior that she could see what she was doing to herself. I wish that I could say that this example is unusual, but unfortunately, it is not. Many people ignore the warning signs from their bodies until they collapse.

Emotional Coping Strategies

If your hardiness is low, it can be difficult to handle even a minor change or stressful event in your life. Strategies that build up your hardiness include building self-esteem, developing assertiveness skills, and learning to communicate your expectations.

To build self-esteem, use the A^3 System from Chapter 6 to change your internal self-talk from negative to positive. To develop assertiveness, try the suggestions from Chapter 6 or go to an assertiveness training class where you will learn the tools and techniques of assertive behavior.

Finally, begin to acknowledge and communicate your expectations. People cannot read our minds, so we need to let others know what we want and expect in any given situation. If you want a promotion, let your boss know. If you expect a certain outcome on a project, discuss it. If you expect to be treated a certain way, let the other person know. Sometimes this is easier said than done, but you can begin by practicing in low-risk situations with people who feel nonthreatening to you to build your confidence. You are the only one who can take care of you.

These inventories will have given you a sense of where you are currently experiencing stress in your life. Perhaps you are experiencing very little. Perhaps, like the woman in the earlier example, you are about to experience full burnout. Unless such information is called to our attention, we tend to ignore it. Use what you have learned about the stress in your life to begin to make changes where they are needed.

Chapter 8 in Review

Stop and think about what you have read and learned in Chapter 8 that is interesting or useful to you. Fill in the diagram of the memory tree in Figure 8-2 with key words that remind you of what you learned. You may first want to write down the two main headings from Chapter 8 on the branches of the tree in Figure 8-2. Then under each branch, add your key words to fill in the details so that you will anchor the information in your memory.

Figure 8-2.
Chapter 8 in review.

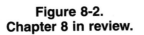

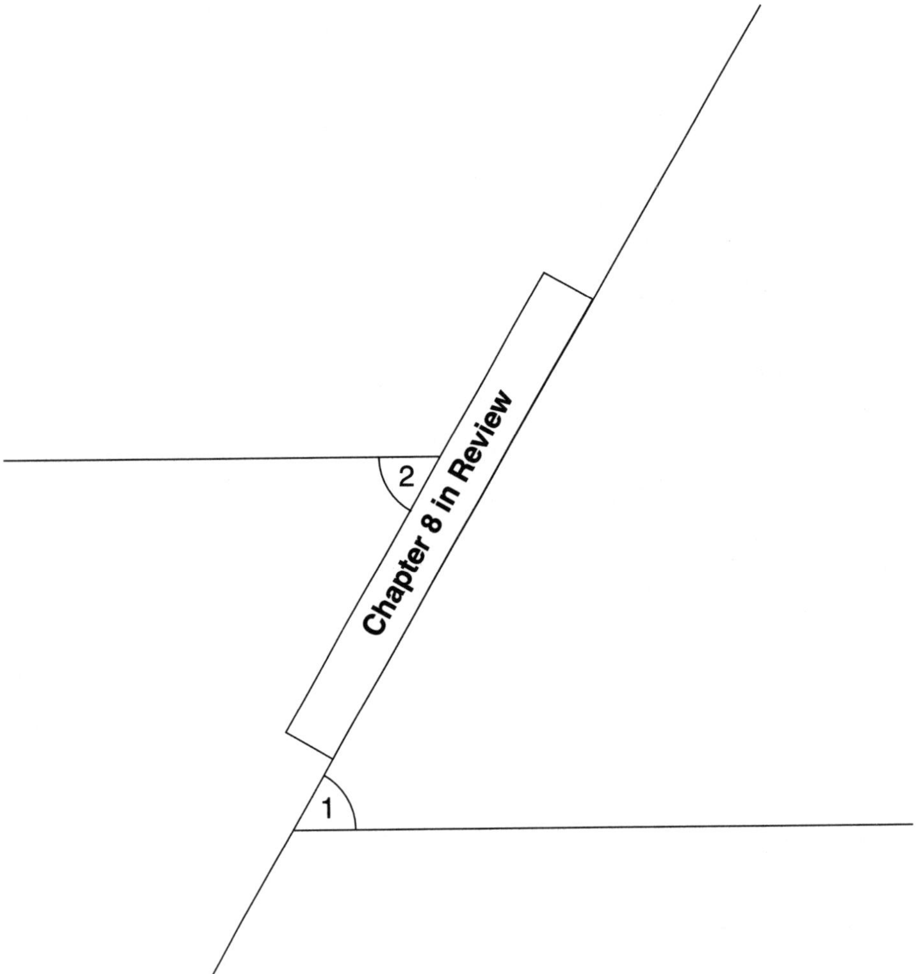

Chapter 8 in Review

2

1

CHAPTER 9

Finding Your
Way to Balance

Preview Points

- Learn how to develop a positive outlook.
- Understand a process to help you when difficult situations arise.
- Explore communication dynamics.
- Learn why you need to continue learning.
- Keep the four facets of your physical, mental, emotional, and spiritual life in check.
- Learn the top-ten tips for maintaining balance.

To achieve and maintain balance, it is important to implement practices in your life that will support you and keep you on track. The following four components can create daily balance in your life.

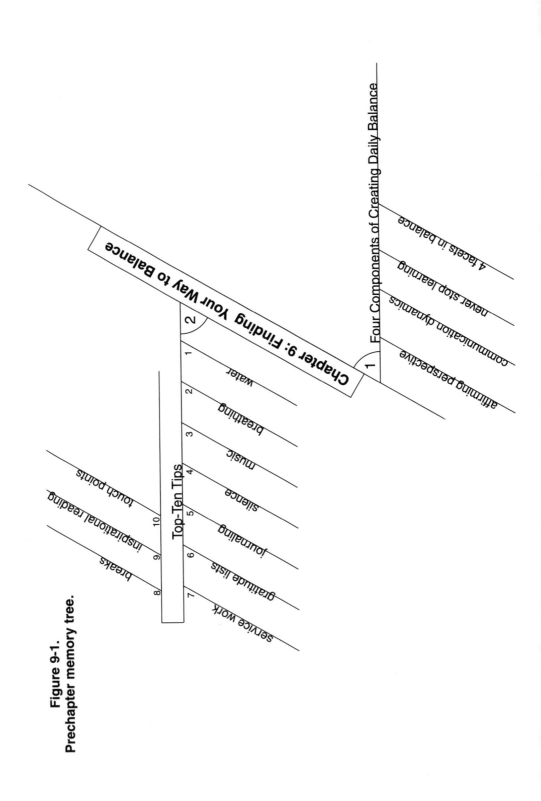

Figure 9-1.
Prechapter memory tree.

Chapter 9: Finding Your Way to Balance

Four Components of Creating Daily Balance

1
- affirming perspective
- communication dynamics
- never stop learning
- 4 facets in balance

2 Top-Ten Tips
1. water
2. breathing
3. music
4. silence
5. journaling
6. gratitude lists
7. service work
8. breaks
9. inspirational reading
10. touch points

Four Components of Creating Daily Balance

1. Maintain an affirming life perspective.

2. Understand communication dynamics.

3. Never stop learning.

4. Keep your physical, mental, emotional, and spiritual lives in balance.

When implemented on a regular basis, these components build a solid foundation for your life that will help you withstand any storms that may arise.

Maintain an Affirming Life Perspective

We are bombarded with negative messages on a regular basis. The news, advertising, cartoons, and perhaps our work atmosphere send out negativity in waves, but we don't need to be caught up in it. It is our approach to life that counts.

There is an old story about three bricklayers. One day, a curious child approaches the bricklayers to see what they are doing. When the child reaches the first bricklayer and asks, "What are you doing?," the bricklayer groans, spits, and wipes his brow as he glances up from his work and says with a grunt, "I'm layin' brick, what does it look like, kid!" The child says, "Oh," and moves on to the next bricklayer. When the child asks the second bricklayer about what he is doing, the bricklayer moans and says with a downcast sigh, "I'm earning a living." The child thanks him and moves on to the third bricklayer. The third bricklayer springs up with a sparkle in his eye and excitement in his voice and says, "I'm building a cathedral!" As the child listens, the bricklayer goes on, with great enthusiasm, to describe the vision that he is a part of.

Which bricklayer are you? When you get up in the morning do you prepare to lay brick in your life and suffer? Or do you feel victimized by the way you earn your living? Or, like the third bricklayer, are you building a cathedral out of your life? The choice is yours. It is a matter of how you approach it.

Three Phases for Dealing with Difficult Situations

A second process for maintaining an affirmative outlook on life is the three-phase system for dealing with difficult situations. The three phases are change, accept, and leave.

When you are faced with a situation in which you are unhappy, you need to take action to resolve the situation or risk becoming a victim of it. Unfortunately, when a situation is very challenging for us, we tend to want to leave it or to ignore it. The risk is that we will repeat the situation over and over again until we deal with it. Matters worsen until we have no option but to leave. And chances are we will get the opportunity to learn the lesson elsewhere.

However, if you are currently in a situation where you are physically or emotionally threatened, or your health is in serious jeopardy from stress, your best course of action may be to leave.

PHASE ONE   Change

When you find yourself in a relationship or job in which you are unhappy, the first step is to change what *you* are doing. Our temptation is to blame the other person or situation, but remember, we always have a part to play. Instead, begin identifying what you can do differently. Teach yourself to respond instead of reacting to what is going on. Work on forgiveness. Focus on what you are grateful for in your life. Let go of resentments. As the saying goes, "Resentments are like taking poison and expecting the other person to die."

Practice this for thirty days. You may find that the situation has resolved itself or no longer has the power to upset you. When you change your responses and attitude about the situation, it is more likely that the other people involved will change, too.

After you have tried your best for thirty days, reevaluate the situation. If you are still dissatisfied, it is time to move on to phase two.

PHASE TWO   Accept

In phase two, you work to accept the situation. Remember that acceptance does not mean that you like, approve of, or agree with what is happening. Acceptance means that you stop struggling against the reality of the way things are. You may think things should be different, but they aren't. (Remember our discussion on *should*'s?) You may wish someone did something differently, but he or she did not. You can let your desires be known, but the other party is not required to change as a result of your request.

For example, I do not make the bed in my home. (I have never made my bed—just ask my mother.) My husband would like me to make the bed every morning and mentions this from time to time (he usually leaves the house early; I tend to sleep in when I'm not on the road). I see no need to make it when it will only become messed up again. I frequently suggest that since he wants to sleep in a made-up bed, *he* make it before he goes to sleep at night. Every once in a while, I make the bed, but most often only when we change the sheets. My husband has learned to accept this. He still thinks I should make the bed, but it doesn't upset him. (Just as it no longer upsets me that he leaves his shoes in the middle of the floor!)

This may seem like a trivial issue to you, but the point is that anything can become a barrier if you let it. What we want often differs from the way things are. We need to learn to let go of some of the struggle we cause in ourselves by realizing that some things just *are* the way they are.

A woman who had attended my program came back to a second program and shared the following experience. She had learned the three phases of change, accept, or leave, which she applied to her relationship with her boss. Her boss liked to holler and bellow about things from his office. Mary, my participant, would become upset every time he did this. She would go home crying on some nights and be miserable for a couple of days afterward. After learning the three-phase process, she changed how she responded to his bellowing. She stopped taking it personally or feeling embarrassed for him. She reported that this helped a great deal in keeping her calm. She no longer became as upset as she used to be. But she still wished he would stop it. She believed that it was inappropriate and unprofessional. (I agree with her.)

However, that is how he chose to behave, and she couldn't change him. Mary worked on accepting his behavior and no longer let it have the power to affect her in the slightest way. She told us what a relief it was to simply ignore him. On some days, she even enjoyed his bellowing, because it gave her a chance to see how silly he was and how strong she felt. Since that program, Mary has kept in touch with me. She told me that she taught the rest of the people in her office the process, and he hardly yells now because no one responds to him.

Try practicing acceptance for thirty days. Then reevaluate your situation. If it is still unacceptable, then it is time for phase three.

PHASE THREE   Leave

Now that you have worked on changing everything you can and accepting the situation as it is, you have begun the process of learning from the situation. If you now find yourself unable to tolerate the situation any longer, it is appropriate to start planning to leave.

Notice I said *planning* to leave, not just leave. Make certain that you have a support system in place, because even though you know you need to do this, it doesn't mean it will be easy. Have people in your life ready to be there for you when you need it. If you will be leaving a relationship, decide beforehand where you will go. If you are going to ask your partner to leave, how will you do it? If you are leaving a job, have another one in place first. Also, plan to discuss with the people involved why you are leaving. Explain what your experience has been and how you have tried to work through your dissatisfaction. Sometimes the other party may become defensive; sometimes you may find yourself renegotiating the situation. You will be surprised at the response you receive when you speak with conviction and calmness about how *you* see things.

If nothing else when you leave, you can be comforted by the fact that you did the best you could. You have learned a great deal about yourself. When you see similar patterns arising in your life again, you will be better equipped to handle them. You are now ready to move on with your life.

Understand Communication Dynamics

Another component of creating daily balance is understanding communication dynamics. We will explore different aspects of communication and discuss skills you can use to be more effective.

One aspect of communication is learning not to take things personally. I think the following sayings can help you with this goal:

- What you think of me is none of my business.

- A person's behavior is a reflection of them, not of me.

- We teach people how to treat us by what we tolerate.

Remembering these three sayings can help you to stay balanced in most situations. Let's take a closer look at each one.

What You Think of Me Is None of My Business

People are entitled to their opinions, just as we are entitled to ours. However, that does not mean we have to accept their opinions or react to them. When someone offers his or her opinion of you—especially when it is negative—avoid defending yourself. Use an assertive phrase such as, "I'll keep that in mind," or "You may be right, tell me more." Then decide whether what they are telling you is helpful or not. If not, let it go.

A great many of us waste too much energy worrying about what others may think or say about us. The truth is that people will do what they do. We don't control them. It is a better use of our energy to focus on the person *we* want to be and take action based on *our* values rather than worrying about living up to someone else's ideals.

People's Behavior Is a Reflection of Them, Not of Me

This saying helps us to remember that we cannot control others and cannot make them do anything. How often have you heard someone say, "You made me angry!" Remember, when people are under stress they sometimes externalize their problems. They blame other people for what is happening in their lives. Don't buy into this. You do not have the power to *make* them do anything. And just think, if you did have that kind of power over someone, would you really use it to make them upset with *you*? I doubt it.

A great example of this is a conversation I had with a colleague named Bryn, who was going through a messy divorce. He shared with me an upsetting conversation he had with his soon-to-be ex-wife. The night before, she had accused him of making her have an affair and move out of their home. Bryn was very upset by her accusation, and was racking his brain to figure out what he had done to make her do this. I shared this saying with him and suggested that he had no control over her choice. I pointed out that even if he did have that control, would he have used it to "make" her have an affair and leave? Of course he would not! Bryn felt much better and began to regain some of his self-esteem by reflecting on these sayings.

We Teach People How to Treat Us by What We Tolerate

This third saying can sometimes be a tough one to swallow. It means that we have a part to play in what we may have viewed in the past as the other person being the bad guy. What I think is great about this saying is that it puts us back in control over how we are treated. If you don't like how you are treated in a given relationship, take a look at what you have been putting up with. Think back to situations and see whether there were times you could have spoken up for yourself but didn't. It is time to start working on those assertiveness skills again. Remember, since you will be changing the pattern of these relationships, you can expect some resistance. People have learned that they can treat you a certain way, and you will be changing that. They will more than likely resist or not believe you when you start to do things differently, but keep at it. Remember that resistance means that things are moving and happening—don't fall back into old patterns because of it.

One example of this is my friend Nina. When she started her job, she was eager to please, so she helped people whenever they asked. As her responsibilities as a manager grew and her workload increased, she started to become resentful of people expecting her to fix the copy machine, make coffee, or get office supplies from the cabinet when they could easily do it themselves. What she forgot was that for two years she had been doing these things joyfully for others. It was *she* who had changed, not them. I coached her to determine which tasks she needed to release. Many of the tasks were the things she had grown in the habit of doing for others. I suggested that she start letting them go one by one, and I cautioned her to expect initial resistance and disappointment from some of her coworkers. I reminded her that she didn't have to give up all these niceties forever, but she needed to change the pattern she had initially created. In time, she could perform these services *once in a while*, as time permitted. When we train people to expect things of us, we are responsible for retraining them when our circumstances change.

Modes of Communication

The final aspect of communication dynamics is to understand the different communication modes and how they operate under stress. Most of us have a preference for one, which can be identified by our behavior. We will briefly discuss the following modes of communication:

- Relator/harmonizer

- Socializer/idealist

- Thinker/preserver

- Director/achiever

There are many books and courses available to you if you wish to explore these dynamics further.

Keep in mind that these are *behaviors*. We all have the capacity to exhibit characteristics of each mode. Under stress, each mode tends to display negative, immature behavior. These behaviors stem from a need to regain balance. By providing what others need under stress it is possible to avoid misunderstandings and conflict. You can also learn *your* needs and communicate them to others so they know how to respond to you when you are anxious.

RELATOR/HARMONIZER Relator/harmonizers are natural communicators and tend to keep their surroundings as comfortable and relaxed as possible. They are peacemakers and mediators. Relator/harmonizers are detail-oriented and excellent listeners. They can be slow to accept change and like to work in group or team environments. When anxious, relator/harmonizers may appear to others to be indecisive, submissive, defensive, or withdrawn. When working with a relator/harmonizer who is under tension, they need reassurance that the problem isn't personal, one-on-one discussion of the issue, and a detailed explanation at a slower pace.

If you are a relator/harmonizer, you can use the following tips to improve your ability to handle stressful situations:

- Learn to confidently say no.

- Learn to delegate and ask for help.

- Accept changes in procedure when they occur.

- Talk to other people about your needs, thoughts, and feelings.

- Avoid taking things personally.

SOCIALIZER/IDEALIST Socializer/idealists are interactive. They enjoy people and tend to be talkative. They are natural negotiators and strategists, and they like attention. Socializer/idealists like things to be fast-paced and exciting. They can have difficulty working alone and tend to be disorganized. Socializer/idealists are people who focus on the big picture.

When anxious, socializer/idealists may appear to others as being manipulative, sarcastic, inconsistent, and impulsive. When working with a socializer/idealist who is under tension, they need to take action and interact with people, a fast pace, recognition, an opportunity to calm down, and assurance of approval.

If you are a socializer/idealist, you can use the following tips to improve your ability to handle stressful situations:

■ Concentrate on the issue at hand.

■ Develop organizational skills.

■ Be sure to complete what you start.

■ Avoid becoming overly emotional.

■ Let other people share the spotlight.

THINKER/PRESERVER Thinker/preservers are analytical. They tend to be detail-oriented and highly organized. Thinker/preservers are thorough and dependable. They are slow-paced and need time to consider options. They like to work alone and appreciate clear and direct communication.

When anxious, thinker/preservers may appear to others as being unimaginative, reclusive, resistant to change, and overly dependant on data. When working with thinker/preservers who are under tension, they need time to ask questions and research information, assurance of accuracy, recognition of their performance, and clear expectations.

If you are a thinker/preserver, you can use the following tips to improve your ability to handle stressful situations:

■ Work on timely decision making.

■ Try to compromise on some issues.

- Use policies and procedures as guidelines, not laws.

- Try utilizing some time-saving tools.

- Remember to acknowledge the work of other people.

DIRECTOR/ACHIEVER Director/achievers are efficiency masters. They are focused on tasks and results. They make quick decisions and are single-minded and focused. Director/achievers get things done and strive for efficiency.

When anxious, director/achievers may appear to others as being impatient, critical, demanding, aggressive, and rude. When working with a director/achiever who is under tension, they need a sense of control, evidence of progress, a goal to work toward and focus on, and reminders that things will work out.

If you are a director/achiever, you can use the following tips to improve your ability to handle stressful situations:

- Take time to talk with people and really listen.

- Acknowledge the efforts of other people.

- Slow down and relax.

- Explain to other people the reasoning behind your decisions.

- Work on becoming more patient and sensitive toward other people.

You can use this information about communication modes as a guide for gaining insight into yourself and those you interact with regularly. It can also help you to not take things personally. We all have our communication preferences that reflect our individual styles. In addition, you can use this information to become more assertive. Use the tips to improve yourself and to understand the communication needs of other people who are under stress.

Never Stop Learning

Component number three to creating balance in your life is to never stop learning. Having an openness to learning, growing, and changing is essential for creating a balanced life.

Learn

Learn something new at least once a week. The learning may be formal or informal, it doesn't matter—just keep exploring your world and seeking new ideas. Learn something new about a loved one, watch your child learn, take a class, read a book, find a new route to work, look up something in the encyclopedia, read a magazine—anything that will broaden your horizons and stop you from becoming stagnant.

I meet many people who feel they are finished with learning once they are out of school. The truth is, we are only beginning at that point. School lays the foundation, however, it is up to us to continue throughout the rest of our lives. I regularly have individuals brag to me that they haven't read a book in ten years or more!

Put learning toward the top of your priority list. When we stop learning, our options narrow and we can feel limited. When you hit a stressful spot in life, all that learning will come in handy to help you find new alternatives.

Learning also helps to broaden our perspectives on life. When we are faced with a great deal of change, our focus can narrow. The more knowledge we have gathered, the more inner support we will have in stressful times.

Grow

It has been said that there are two ways in which we grow: one is through pain and the other is though conscious effort.

Sometimes the pains of life are unavoidable. We lose those we care about. Awful accidents happen. We are out of work. If these events occur, we need a support system, daily ritual, and a source of hope to help us though.

However, some of the pains of life are avoidable. When we have been living out of balance for an extended period of time, life tends to become painful. The pain is usually so minor at first that we tend to ignore it. We ignore pains such as headaches and backaches, stomach problems, irritability, impatience, and problems in communication. These, as you read about earlier, are the early warning signs of burnout.

When we don't take action in the early stages, the pain increases and intensifies. The pain may or may not be physical. When we are not taking care of ourselves and have not set a direction or purpose in life, we can feel like we are victims of our circumstances.

Some of the obvious pains we see are the mid-life crises of people who never took the time—or felt they had a chance—to find out who they were, stress-induced heart attacks and ulcers, surprise separations and divorces, and the sudden loss of a job in which we thought we were being effective.

All of these are avoidable when we take the time to pause in life and figure out who we are and what we truly want. By having a vision for our lives and working toward that vision, we can avoid the pain these harsh lessons bring.

This brings us to the second way we grow, which is through conscious effort. When we are life-long learners, have a sense of purpose, and have concrete goals, we tend to make conscious choices and decisions. By utilizing the techniques that you have read about in this book and consistently applying them, you are growing. Even if you only have the awareness that you *can* do something different to get better results out of your life, reading this book has served a valuable purpose.

To grow consciously instead of through pain, follow the three-step process of taking inventory, setting goals, and taking regular action.

1. *Take a personal inventory.* You may start with the life audit or stress inventories from this book or simply think about the many roles you play in your life and how satisfied you are with them.

2. *Set goals.* Once you have a sense of how you currently see

your life, decide how you want to improve it. Determine the outcomes you want in these areas of your life and set short- and long-term goals to achieve those outcomes.

3. *Take regular action.* On a daily or weekly basis, take some kind of action to move you closer to your goals. Remember to give this time and have patience. You are building your life, and lives are not built in a day.

Change

Once in a while do something different. Change the way you wear your hair, the way you dress, the way you drive to work—any routine thing will do. Allow yourself to experiment with your life. You never know when you will discover something that is better suited to you. Change of this nature keeps things new, fresh, and alive. I am not suggesting you take up bungee jumping—unless that is your style. Just begin to explore your regular habits and routines to see where you may be in a rut and not know it. If what you try isn't for you, that is okay. You still learned something new about yourself, and at least you tried. Change can help you to know yourself better. If you invite your friends, loved ones, or coworkers to experiment with you, you can get to know each other better, too!

Keep Your Four Facets in Balance

Another way to create balance in your life is to keep your four facets in balance. Undertake a weekly facet review to monitor your activities. Once a week, review how well you have performed in the areas of physical, mental, emotional, and spiritual care.

Physical care simply means to reflect on how well you took care of your body. Did you get any exercise? Did you get enough rest? Did you make decent choices about eating? If not, determine what you will do the following week to improve. I don't suggest you exhaust yourself with exercise or go on a crash diet because these can feel like punishment. Instead, decide to take the stairs when you can, determine to go to bed earlier or take a nap, or make healthy snacks for yourself to have at home and at work. Start small and work your way up. As your physical health improves, you will feel increasingly motivated to make positive changes.

Mental care refers to managing your information overload and maintaining a positive and learning attitude. Did you use effective techniques to wade though the data in your life? Are you monitoring your thoughts and canceling those that are negative? Did you learn anything new? Did you take action toward a goal or attempt a change? If not, think about what you can do in the coming week to improve. A positive mental attitude is a powerful mental balancing tool. Again, think small steps. You do not want to overload yourself, rather you are looking for slow, steady progress.

Emotional care is honoring your feelings and expressing them appropriately. Did you speak up when something was important to you? Did you express your emotions (even in writing) when you felt them? Did you express your desires when asked? If not, start paying attention to where you withhold your feelings and begin releasing them, either physically by stretching and moving or by writing out what you feel. Unexpressed emotions can build up and later be expressed as illnesses. Practice acknowledging how you feel, if only to your mirror.

Spiritual care reminds you of your important place in the scheme of things and gives you sustaining hope in the positive nature of life. Did you notice the beauty around you? Did you acknowledge the perfection of you and others in your life? Did you lend a helping hand when it was needed? If not, determine to do so in the coming week. Stop and notice nature. Acknowledge others in a positive way. Honor yourself for working to create a happy life.

When you perform this review, it is important to look for opportunities to improve. Do not beat up on yourself for what you did not do. The focus is always on progressive improvement.

The Top-Ten Tips for Creating Balance

The top-ten tips to finding your way to balance are simple, yet highly effective, techniques that you can implement at any time, almost anywhere, and with no special equipment required.

TIP ONE *Water*

Drink water. How much? The recommended daily amount is six to eight eight-ounce glasses a day. Water keeps our bodies hydrated and improves the condition of our hair and skin. It can improve our eyesight, digestion, and sleep. These are only a few examples of the benefits of water. It is especially important for those of you who drink a large amount of coffee, tea, or colas. These contain caffeine, which can dehydrate us. It has been recommended that we drink an *extra* glass of water for each serving that contains caffeine or artificial sweeteners. This means in addition to the recommended amount. We need this to flush out the toxins these drinks place into our system.

An easy way to ensure that you drink enough is to get a large bottle of water (1.5 liters = approximately six eight-ounce servings), fill it up in the morning, and make certain that it is finished by the end of the day. Over time, you may even wish to increase the amount.

TIP TWO *Breathing*

Breathing is automatic, yet we tend to breathe in a very shallow manner that doesn't provide our bodies with the maximum amount of oxygen. Oxygen is needed for optimum brain function as well as overall health. Taking a few slow, deep breaths not only oxygenates you, it helps you to relax and reset your thinking.

To begin a deep breath, exhale until you feel your diaphragm muscles tighten. Then slowly begin filling up your lungs from the bottom up, like you are inflating a balloon. Once you reach the top of your inhale, pause a second and try to take in just a bit more air. This will help to stretch your lung capacity, allowing you to get even more oxygen into your blood stream. Then slowly exhale, tightening your diaphragm at the bottom of your breath. Repeat this three to four times. On your fourth breath, you will notice the muscles deep in your chest and belly start to open and relax—this is your goal. We hold a lot of tension here and we want to release it.

You will be surprised at how much more relaxed deep breathing will keep you throughout your day.

TIP THREE *Music*

Listen to music to help you de-stress and stay in balance. Use the baroque music mentioned in Part 1 to help you to relax and work more efficiently. Play it at the office and in your car.

Listen to your favorite sing-a-long music to relieve excess tension. Sing at the top of your lungs and let the music move through you. Or dance and move your body to relieve tightness.

TIP FOUR *Silence*

Learn to quiet your mind. Many people are uncomfortable with silence. They find it disturbing to have all their feelings and suppressed thoughts come to the surface.

If this is true for you, you may want to take a class in yoga, meditation, or martial arts. All of these disciplines teach you how to quiet your mind.

Spend some quiet time every morning to prepare for your day. Take a moment before you get out of your car to focus on your next activity. Pause and get quiet throughout your day to keep you focused on your priorities.

TIP FIVE *Journaling*

Spend some time writing about your life. Writing in a journal helps you to understand your world and your place in it. It is a safe place to release your thoughts and feelings.

You may wish to write daily or weekly, but schedule a time to make it routine for you. Don't worry about spelling, grammar, or neatness. Buy yourself a journal that you like the look and feel of, so that it feels special and important to write in. Get a unique pen or pencil that you use only for writing in your journal.

TIP SIX Gratitude Lists

Gratitude lists can dramatically change your life for the better. They help you to refocus how you see the world.

It is easy to start the process. Every night, write down at least three things you are grateful for from that day. (This is a great use for your journal.) At first, it may be difficult and you may find yourself writing things like, "I'm grateful I didn't tell my boss to go to *#!#," or "I'm grateful that I'm still breathing." That is okay to start, but you will soon find many other things to be grateful for. In time, you will begin to see the world from the perspective of gratitude and your lists can become quite long at the end of the day. What a wonderful way to send yourself to sleep!

TIP SEVEN Service Work

Find opportunities to help others. When you perform an act of service, you receive more than you give. It may not feel like it, but it is true.

Start small. Hold the door open for someone in need. Let a car into the stream of traffic in front of you. Do a household chore without being reminded or without reminding others that you did it.

Then graduate. Volunteer in your community to help others.

TIP EIGHT Breaks

Allow yourself to take breaks throughout your day. You will feel more rested and actually be more productive when you allow yourself to take quick breaks. Get up from your desk and take a short walk. Go outside and get some fresh air. Let your eyes, mind, and body relax for a couple of minutes.

TIP NINE Inspirational Reading

Have reading material available at home and work that inspires you. There are many books and daily calendars to choose from.

Get a daily quote book and put it where you will see it often. Try reading inspirational real-life, short story books. Anything that will help to keep you uplifted and act as a positive reminder during your busy day.

TIP TEN *Touch Points*

Touch points are anything you place around you as reminders of what is important to you. They can be pictures of family and friends. Postcards of places you've visited, or plan to visit. Touch points are also cards people have sent you or sayings you have cut out. They can be figurines or toys.

The principle behind touch points is to have things in your environment that uplift you when you see them. They are also there to act as reminders to take action toward your goals.

You can also set up a touch-point system to remind you of things you want to do, but tend to forget in the business of the day. For example, I have a friend who places small blue stickers around her workspace to remind her to pause, take a few deep breaths, and drink some water. Whenever her eyes land on one of these stickers, she remembers to do these things.

I hope you find these tips useful, doable, and practical. Set a goal to begin implementing at least one of them today. Notice the improvement in your life as a result. Then add another, and another . . . As you continue to do self-care amidst the chaos of your environment, your life will grow more and more into balance.

Chapter 9 in Review

Stop and think about what you have read and learned in Chapter 9 that is interesting or useful to you. Fill in the diagram of the memory tree in Figure 9-2 using key words that remind you of what you learned. You may first want to write down the two main headings from Chapter 9 on the branches of the tree in Figure 9-2. Then under each branch, add your key words to fill in the details so that you will anchor the information in your memory.

**Figure 9-2.
Chapter 9 in review.**

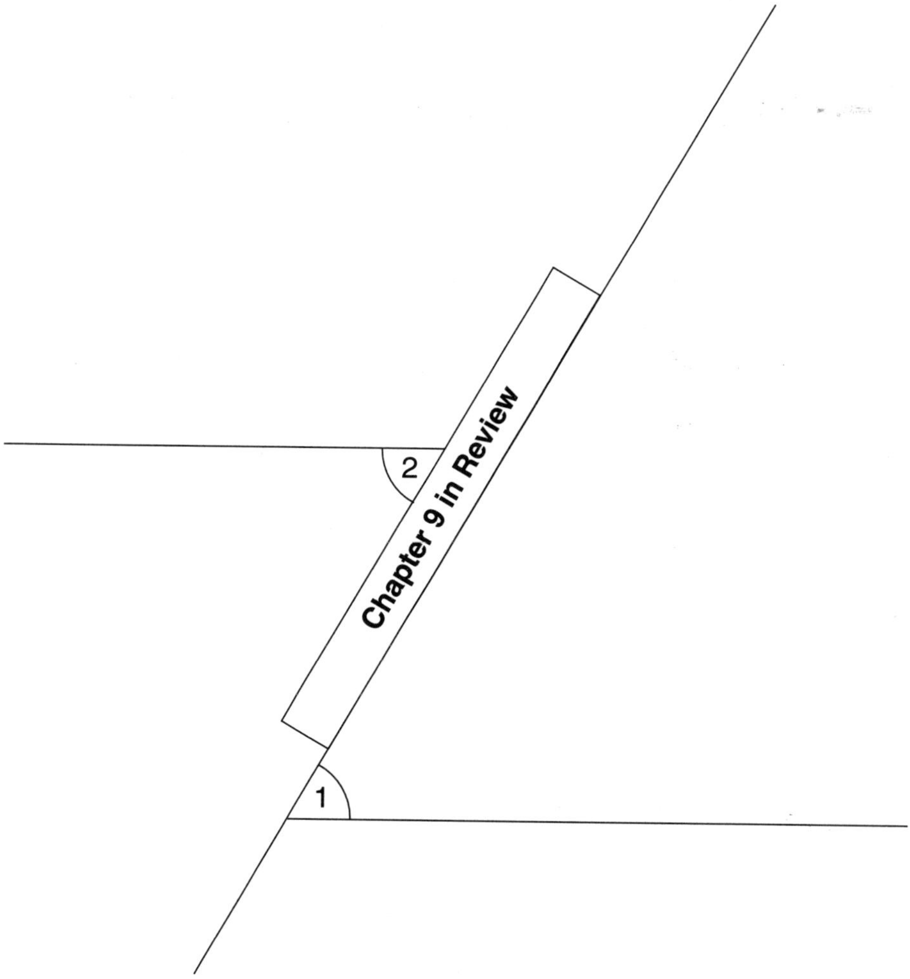

Chapter 9 in Review

CHAPTER 10

Application
Strategies

As you read through this book, you had an opportunity to look at your work and your life from many different perspectives. You determined your current reading rate and learned many techniques for improving your ability to handle information. You looked at how you use your time and how organized you keep your space. You looked at your values and how they are—or are not—reflected in your work. You have gotten a chance to look at the stressors in your life and the support systems that are either in place or absent.

By now, you have a clear picture of where you stand in the cycle of burnout. Most of us are so busy running in place that we don't have a chance to look at our unique big picture. At this point, you have. So, what do you do with it?

One thing I would suggest is that you step back and see whether you are actually where you want to be in your life. From your values identification profile, you have learned what is important to you. We often think that money is important, but once we have enough for our basic needs, money is not necessarily a strong value. Many people find themselves in jobs that pay well but provide little satisfaction. Yet, because of the pay, they feel trapped. This is the perfect formula for burnout.

Spending our days in a cubical when we prefer the out-of-doors, working with machines when we love animals, working with children when we prefer the company of adults (or vice-versa), working in a team when we would much rather work alone—all of these are situations that can be altered when we become aware of our preferences. We can set goals and make changes.

Then again, perhaps you love what you do—but because of that, you do too much of it. Here is another scenario for burnout.

As playwright and poet William Shakespeare wrote, "To thine own self be true, and it must follow as night the day, thou canst not then be false to any man."[1] The more you know about yourself, the better you will be able to decide where you want to go and what you want to do. You may want to make great changes or small ones. The first step is to get your life in order so that you have the information and space to decide.

Let us review what we have learned.

Review

We have explored skills and techniques in three major areas: Information, time, and stress. What percentage of the time do you feel the effects of chaos in these areas?

Information: _____ %

Time: _____ %

Stress: _____ %

Based on this information, begin to consider where you will need to focus your attention in the coming weeks and months to see improvement. Remember to take small steps. Trying to do too much at once will only throw you further into chaos.

Part Review

Figures 10-1 through 10-3 contain memory trees for the three parts of this book. To complete them, go back and review your memory tree from each chapter, and think about what was most useful to you. Then fill in some key words for yourself on the memory tree provided.

Plan and Apply

After reviewing the key points you learned from each part, it is time to set your goals and to begin to put them into action. Remember to write each goal out and make sure that it fits the criteria laid out in Part 2. A method that I find useful for setting and monitoring goals is a goal-planning chart.

Table 10-1 shows a goal chart completed by a participant in one of my seminars. This example is from a man who was having a difficult time asserting himself. He was sent to my course by his boss to learn to "shape up." He wasn't certain what that meant, but came to realize that assertiveness was his first step. At first, his goal was to be an assertive communicator. We worked on that goal and ensured that it conformed to successful goal-setting criteria.

Table 10-2 is a blank for you to use to start your process of removing chaos from your life. Where do you want to go? What would you like to shift in your life? Start with a small goal or something immediate in which you can see quick results. After you have mastered the process, there are no limits to what goals you can reach. Wherever you are in the cycle of burnout, the cycle can stop here.

Whether you have filled in the grid or simply set new intentions, take out a calendar and determine some weekly benchmarks for monitoring your progress over the next thirty to forty-five days. At the end of this time, reevaluate. Have you taken steps to reach your goal? Have you learned that you need to change direction? Is your goal complete? If so, it is time to celebrate and plan your next step. No matter which of these alternatives you have reached, acknowledge yourself for taking action on creating the life you want. Don't let this opportunity to celebrate slip by.

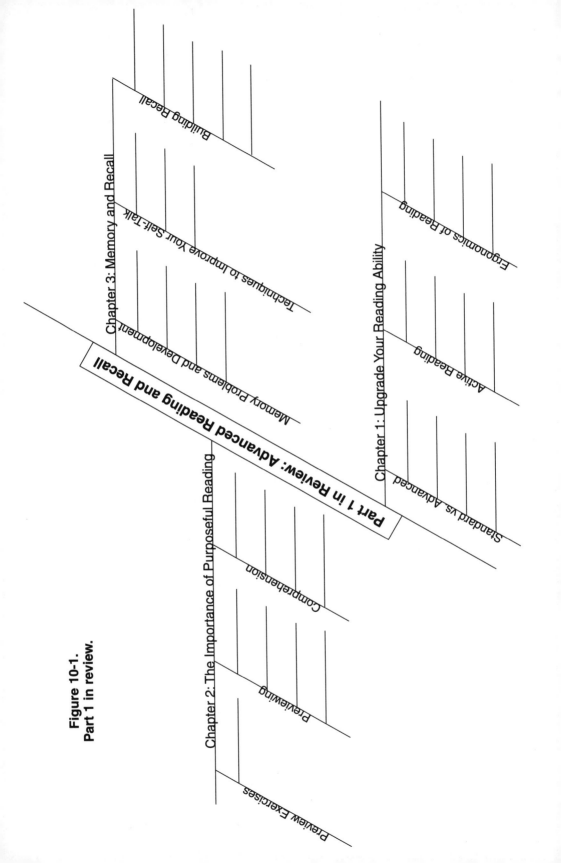

Figure 10-1.
Part 1 in review.

Part 1 in Review: Advanced Reading and Recall

Chapter 1: Upgrade Your Reading Ability
- Standard vs. Advanced
- Active Reading
- Ergonomics of Reading

Chapter 2: The Importance of Purposeful Reading
- Preview Exercises
- Previewing
- Comprehension

Chapter 3: Memory and Recall
- Memory Problems and Development
- Techniques to Improve Your Self-Talk
- Building Recall

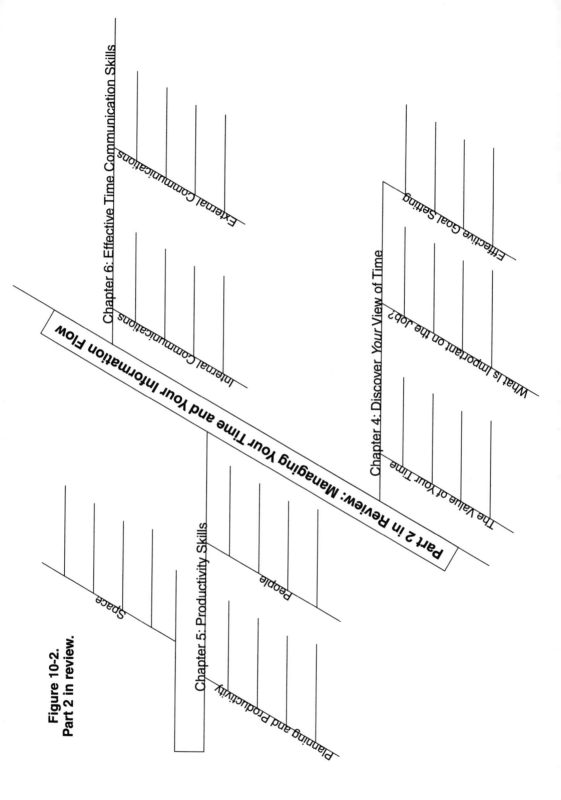

**Figure 10-2.
Part 2 in review.**

Figure 10-3.
Part 3 in review.

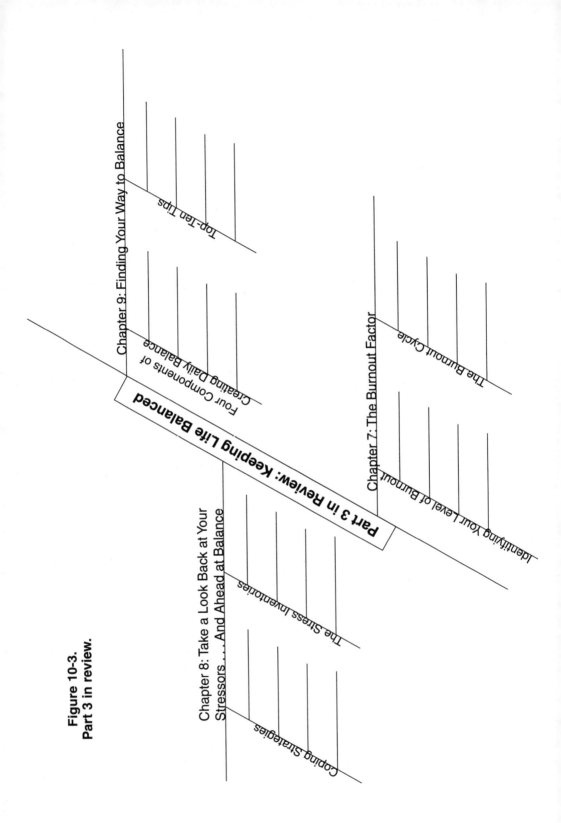

Part 3 in Review: Keeping Life Balanced

Chapter 7: The Burnout Factor
- The Burnout Cycle
- Identifying Your Level of Burnout

Chapter 8: Take a Look Back at Your Stressors . . . And Ahead at Balance
- The Stress Inventories
- Coping Strategies

Chapter 9: Finding Your Way to Balance
- Four Components of Creating Daily Balance
- Top-Ten Tips

Table 10-1.
Example goal chart.

	How I will think differently.	How I will act differently.	How I will feel as a result of positive change.
My Goal: To be an assertive communicator.	I will correct my self-talk when it is negative.	I will give myself time to think when I need it. I will speak clearly and directly.	I will feel self-assured and not let other people's negativity defeat me.
How I will begin to work toward my goal.	I will not assume the worst in my communication situations.	I will know what I want and need in a given situation, not realize it afterward.	I will feel empowered and motivated to keep using my new skills.
Activities I will stop or minimize to accomplish my goal.	I will stop thinking like a victim. I will not automatically put other people's needs before my own.	I will remove any physical barriers between myself and others when communicating.	I will feel relieved and confident.
How I will recognize resistance— In myself: and/or From others:	My resistance will most likely be in the form of self-talk—telling myself "It's not worth it." I will notice others being taken aback when I begin to speak up for myself.	I will not apologize or back down from others.	I will combat my inner resistance with the A^3 System. I will remind myself of my positive affirmations.
What are the risks associated with my accomplishing this goal?	At first I may feel selfish. I may worry about what other people think.	I may go a bit overboard.	I will remind myself that I am making progress.
What are the benefits associated with my accomplishing this goal?	I will get more of what I want from my life.	I will walk taller and look people in the eye.	I will feel less frustrated and see positive results in my relationships.

Table 10-2.
Goal chart.

My Goal:	How I will think differently.	How I will act differently.	How I will feel as a result of positive change.
How I will begin to work toward my goal.			
Activities I will stop or minimize to accomplish my goal.			
How I will recognize resistance— In myself: and/or From others:			
What I will do to deal with any resistance.			
What are the risks associated with my accomplishing this goal?			
What are the benefits associated with my accomplishing this goal?			

P.S.

If you have gained new skills and insights that you can integrate into your workday, then my goal in writing this book has been accomplished. My hope is that you will use these ideas to find greater satisfaction in your work and to create a well-balanced life.

In her book *A Passion for the Possible*, internationally renowned scholar, philosopher, and teacher Jean Houston asks this question, "What would you be like if you started today to make the most of the rest of your life?"[1]

What would you do? How would it feel? Shut your eyes and let yourself take in the expansiveness of the idea. What *would* you be like if you started today to make the most of the rest of your life?

Reading Drill Log

READING DRILL LOG

Date and Time	Word per minute rate (wpm)	Name of material drill conducted in	Comprehension Comments

Endnotes

Chapter 1

1. *Webster's College Dictionary* (New York: Random House, 1991).

2. Howard Stephen Berg, *Super Reading Secrets* (New York: Warner Books, 1992).

3. Sheila Ostrander and Lynn Schroeder, *Super-Learning 2000* (New York: Delacorte Press, 1994).

Chapter 2

1. Donald H. Weiss, *Improve Your Reading Power* (New York: AMACOM, 1988).

2. Peter Russell, *The Brain Book* (New York: Penguin, 1979).

3. John Locke, *The Conduct of the Understanding* (1706).

Chapter 4

1. Tom Peters, *The Pursuit of Wow!* (New York: Random House, Inc., 1994).

Chapter 5

1. Alec Mackenzie, *The Time Trap* (New York: AMACOM, 1997).

2. Merrill E. Douglass, *ABC Time Tips* (New York: McGraw-Hill, 1998).

3. Herbert Victor Prochnow, *The Public Speaker's Treasure Chest: A Compendium of Source Material to Make Your Speech Sparkle* (New York: Harper & Brothers, 1942).

4. Merrill E. Douglass, *ABC Time Tips* (New York: McGraw-Hill, 1998).

Chapter 7

1. Ayala Pines and Elliot Aronson, *Career Burnout: Causes and Cures* (New York: The Free Press, 1988).

Chapter 8

1. Hans Selye, *Stress Without Distress* (New York: Signet, 1974).

2. Ibid.

Chapter 10

1. William Shakespeare, *Hamlet,* in *The Complete Works of Shakespeare* (Reading, Mass.: Addison-Wesley, 1997).

P.S.

1. Jean Houston, *A Passion for the Possible* (New York: HarperCollins, 1997).

Recommended Reading

Berg, Howard Stephen. *Super Reading Secrets*. New York: Warner Books, 1992.

Bromley, Karen, Linda Irwin Vitis, and Marcia Modlo. *Graphic Organizers*. New York: Scholastic, 1995.

Buzan, Tony. *Use Both Sides of Your Brain*. New York: Plume, 1991.

Covey, Stephen R., A. Roger Merrill, and Rebecca R. Merrill. *First Things First*. New York: Simon and Schuster, 1994.

Davis, Martha, Elizabeth Robbins Eshelman, and Matthew McKay. *The Relaxation and Stress Reduction Workbook*. Oakland, CA: New Harbinger Publications, 1998.

Douglass, Merrill. *ABC Time Tips*. New York: McGraw-Hill, 1998.

Fischer, Arron. "Is Your Career Killing You?," *Data Communications*, February 1998.

Frank, Stanley D. *The Evelyn Wood Seven-Day Speed Reading and Learning Program*. New York: Barnes & Noble, 1994.

Grimsley, Kirsten Downey. "Message Overload Taking Toll on Workers," *Washington Post*, May 20, 1998.

Houston, Jean. *A Passion for the Possible*. New York: Harper-Collins Publishers Inc., 1997.

Kluger, Jeffrey. "The Battle to Save Your Memory," *Time*, June 12, 2000.

Kump, Peter. *Break-Though Rapid Reading*. Paramus, NJ: Prentice Hall Press, 1999.

Moidel, Steve. *Speed Reading for Business*. Hauppauge, NY: Barron's Business Books, 1998.

Morgenstern, Julie. *Organizing from the Inside Out*. New York: Henry Holt and Company, 1998.

Newman, John. *Wisdom for Earthlings*. New York: AMACOM, 1996.

Ostrander, Sheila, and Lynn Schroeder. *Super-Learning 2000*. New York: Delacorte Press, 1994.

Peterson, Karen. "Why Everyone Is So Short Tempered," *USA Today*, July 18, 2000.

Rinke, Wolf J. *The Six Success Strategies for Winning at Life, Love & Business*. Deerfield Beach, FL: Heath Communications Inc., 1996.

Rosenfeld, Jill. "Want to Lead Better? It's Simple," *Fast Company*, March 2000.

Rosner, Bob. *Working Wounded*. New York: Warner Books, 1998.

Schneider, Sunny. *Improve Your Vision*. Salem, OR: Unique Perspectives Press, 2001.

Scholl, Lisette. *28 Days to Reading Without Glasses: A Natural Method for Improving Your Vision*. Secaucus, NJ: Carol Publishing Group, 1998.

Selye, Hans. *Stress Without Distress*. New York: Signet, 1974.

Shenk, David. "Why You Feel the Way You Do," *Inc.*, January 1999.

Veninga, Robert L., and James P. Spradley. *The Work Stress Connection*. New York: Ballantine Books, 1981.

Wheeler, Liza. "Control the Chaos," *National Institute of Business Management*, Special Report 289, February 1999.

Wurman, Richard Saul. *Information Anxiety*. New York: Bantam Books, 1990.

_____. "De-Stress, De-Fuse, Re-Charge," *Executive Female*, August 2000.

_____. "Skills for Success," *Soundview Executive Book Summaries*, 1989.

_____. "*The Emerging Digital Economy II*," U.S. Department of Commerce, June 1999.

Index

About the Author

Patricia J. Hutchings is a dynamic and talented presenter who is committed to helping people find value in their lives and in the workplace. The emphasis in her programs is on empowerment. Hutchings believes in the inherent abilities of all her participants and skillfully facilitates their process of self-discovery. She has conducted intensive personal and professional development programs for more than sixty-five thousand people in fourteen countries.

For more information about Patricia J. Hutchings's programs or to order a reading-drill tape or music for learning, contact:

Unique Perspectives Un-Limited, Inc.

Web site: www.upunlimited.com

Telephone: (503) 361-8797

Fax: (503) 361-1285

E-mail: patriciah@upunlimited.com